Steven Milner Learns Rhythm Guitar

Learn guitar as you would with your friends

3rd edition

by

Andrew Milner

Find me on Instagram: @andrewmilnermusic

Even more about me: https://linktr.ee/AndrewMilner

Cover illustration artist: https://www.fiverr.com/meow_bug

TABLE OF CONTENTS

Chapter 1 - The birthday gift

It was the morning of May 24th. The sun shone down on the raindrops from the night before, giving everything a splendid shine. Steven Milner, a 14-year-old, long-haired boy, was playing video games with his twin brother, Adrian. They were really focused on their activity because after all, he who won that football game was to gain bragging rights until the next one. Their excitement was high due to the next day's events as well.

'So, what do you think we'll be doing tomorrow?' asked Steven.

'I don't know, I don't have access to that part of the book', replied Adrian.

'Access to the…what now?' a bewildered Steven asked.

'It's…you know what, never mind, let's just leave it at I don't know.'

When looking at the two boys, you'd be hard-pressed to believe they were twins. Steven always enjoyed looking after himself, so you would almost always find him wearing a shirt, his hair combed from top to bottom, and with his sunglasses ever present. Adrian, on the other hand, preferred his hair short and his clothes as easy to maintain as possible, which is why you'd almost always find him in a grey t-shirt, which was his current attire, having changed it from his previous one of wearing white t-shirts. He believed in focusing his energy elsewhere, which, for now, was to win this game.

'Anyway', continued Steven. 'I was wondering more about what you think we'll be getting for our birthdays. I tried looking through the browser history on our parents' laptop, but all I could find were some conveniently placed searches regarding how parents can convince their children to do something other than play video games all day. Do you think they're trying to tell us something?'

'Hm…', Adrian said while thinking to himself. With him having played piano since the age of four, he had hoped he would be able to convince his brother to learn an instrument as well. He even started to learn guitar at the age of seven. Their parents always told Adrian that someday, Steven would be curious enough to want to learn an instrument, but so far, this hasn't happened.

'Maybe they'll get you an instrument so you could start spending your time playing it instead of games. Pretty sure there's a hint in the title of this book we're a part of, but I can't access that either', he then added.

'I always love it when you start glitching like that, though you do sound like a robot trying to act human', remarked Steven.

'What can I say? I live to not care too much about how I am perceived by other people'

Steven then continued his original train of thought.

'Given the strategic deletion of any and all web searches with regards to gifts...that or browsing in incognito...I am guessing it is a bigger surprise than usual. You may just get your wish, though I always considered myself fit for other roles. A singer, for example'.

'I sort of get where you are coming from, though that would imply you taking singing lessons, being able to hold a note for more than half a second and losing the shyness'.

'Ah, yes, out of the two of us, I am the shy one, not the one who spends the first 10 minutes of a conversation over-analyzing every detail about everyone', replied Steven.

'It's called learning who you're dealing with and figuring out any potential weaknesses in them. For example, thanks to this conversation, you now have a canyon in your defences', said Adrian, who then managed to score the winning goal of their match.

'HA! I win.'

'Where I come from, that's called cheating. And being annoying', replied Steven.

'We literally live in the same house! Anyhow, up for a snack?'

Steven groaned, but the two decided to take a break and went to the kitchen to see if there were any snacks lying about.

'Bleh, no sweets apparently', said Steven.

'Nah, just some fruit. Oh well, I'm hungry, and they say apples keep doctors away so…'

After eating some apples, Steven went back to the whole singing debate:

'You know, I wouldn't mind knowing how to play an instrument or sing. It's just that I never really had any motivating factor to help keep me focused enough or determined enough to do it'.

'Well, there's that whole high school band contest that happens every year'.

'What, you mean the one between the first four high schools that were built in the city? Don't children's families start prepping their kids for it from like the first half a second after they're born?'

'Yeah, but those people rarely win, funnily enough. They get burnt out and fail', replied Adrian.

'And you know this how?'

'By seeing how many people from our class and school were determined to be the very best, like no one before them ever was, a year ago. And how many remain in that race. I'd estimate at least half of them have dropped out of the preparations so far. At least from what I gather from conversations'

'You actually have conversations with other people?', a bemused Steven asked.

'Not with a lot of people, but those that talk to me do have conversations with other people. Funnily enough, they also like to confide in me. I guess they figure I'm not a loud-mouth by nature so they feel safe or something.'

Steven pondered for a bit, then added:

'It feels weird because I remember you having a beef with two classmates because you kept telling on everyone to our homeroom teacher when she asked you'

'Oh, that was just petty vengeance for when those 2 girls, dubbed the smart ones, left me out to dry once in biology and I got an F for it.'

'That…makes sense. Anyhow, tell me more about this battle thing. What's it about and how does it work?'

'It happens in 11th grade, junior year of high school basically. And since we're just finishing eighth grade now, that gives us like three years to get in shape for it. Plus, people usually train for this not knowing exactly what bands they're supposed to play.'

'Oh right, because it only involves cover versions, except for the years it doesn't I guess. Doesn't everyone find out the bands they're supposed to cover in like ninth grade or something to have an unnecessarily long year and a half till high-school band selection day to practice?' asked Steven.

'Yeah, people are nuts about this because they have the distinct impression it means something in life if you win it. Though with us leaning more towards Andrew Gordon High School, which hasn't won it in almost two decades, it looks like we don't have to worry too much about it' replied Adrian.

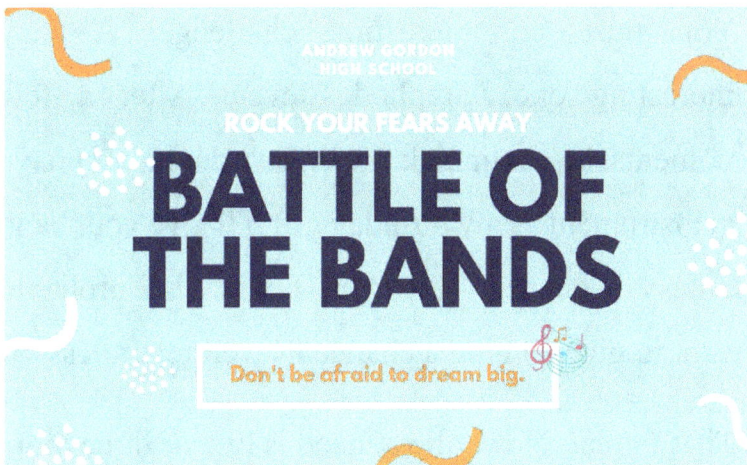

'Huh...almost two decades, eh?' asked Steven with an intrigued look on his face.

'Yeah. But seriously, are you down for this? I mean, if you do get a musical instrument as a present. Would you feel like learning to play it well enough so we could compete at this contest?'

Steven gave it a moment's thought. Something about that huge amount of time with their future high-school choice had intrigued him. What if he and his brother had been the ones to finally end the drought? People would write so much about it. He would be adored and talked about for years.

'You raise an interesting challenge. A very interesting one...' replied Steven. After a few moments, he continued: 'Yeah, let's do this. If I have an instrument as my birthday gift, I'll give your band fantasy a chance. However, I will also probably want to give singing a chance as well regardless.'

'That's great. Now, all we need is two or three more members, and we're all set. No idea where to find any of them though…'.

Sunday arrived, and both the boys were ecstatic. The Milners were not a particularly wealthy family, but they did pretty well, what with managing to keep their monthly expenses at a very low amount.

Sure, you'd never really see them dressed in highly expensive brands or driving extremely expensive cars, but their philosophy, one which they tried to instill in their children as well, is that you don't need the most expensive gear to get the job done. You just need to be able to work smart and hard towards your goals.

And when their parents entered their room, wishing them Happy Birthday, they finally got to unwrap their presents. Adrian got two T-Shirts, one with his favorite racing driver and one with his (and Steven's) favorite anime.

Steven received what he noted was his Godfather's guitar. Steven was really, really happy with this gift, almost so that he didn't recognize himself. 'Huh, this is a new feeling. Maybe I am more interested in this than I originally thought', he thought to himself.

'Listen, we know that telling a 14-year-old to not play video games all day long is like attempting to talk to a wall', said Steven's father, Aaron. 'We thought that since you like spending so much time with your brother, playing an instrument would be the ideal activity for you'.

'And we don't want to hear you say you want to quit practicing after one week', said Allison, the boys' mother. 'We want you to learning for at least the summer break. If afterwards you feel like it's not for you, we'll discuss other options then and there'.

The rest of the day went on pretty smoothly. Steven, while eager to start learning how to play the guitar, figured that since today is his birthday, no one would mind another day of video games, which turned out to be true. However, as he went to sleep that night, he thought that tomorrow, after school, was the best time to get accustomed to his new friend.

Chapter 2 - Steven Milner and his new guitar friend

'I wonder, if this was a race, and the clock was part of it, if the clock got those blue flags, will it move faster or just get out of the way? And if it did get out of the way, would time move faster or just stand still, making everyone forever trapped in this never-ending discussion about who knows what. Man, I am bored…', Steven thought to himself as the literature teacher kept talking about what she thought some author meant by some random poem line.

He was not a Monday person by any means, and he seemed to have understood why no one ever created a more lighthearted song about the annoyance that is Monday. Nevertheless, it was the final class of the day, which meant only one thing. There were only 30 minutes (which felt like days) left till he could finally go home and start figuring out how guitars function.

The guitar he received was a classical one, which belonged to his Godfather, who decided to pass it on since he didn't really feel like playing it anymore. He always cited some "I'm too old for this stuff" reason, but Steven always suspected that it was because he didn't really like playing it in the first place.

The instrument was kept in very good shape though, the brown paint job still shining after all these years. Steven also received a set of new strings along with the guitar, which was a relief since he noticed that the strings the guitar came with sounded muffled.

After what seemed like a millennium, the class ended. Steven almost reached peak human condition when he started packing his belongings. To say he was excited would be an understatement. It didn't help that Adrian, being a methodical person, always liked to arrange his belongings in his backpack in a certain order.

'You're doing this on purpose aren't you?', Steven asked.

'Yes. Also, we are only a 15-minute walk away from home, we'll get there soon', replied Adrian.

On their walk home, Steven asked:

'So, you've been playing the guitar for like seven years now, right? Is it hard to learn?'

'No, it's easy, compared to the piano at least. The answer also depends, of course, on what you want to learn. Playing rhythm guitar is very different than playing lead guitar and both of them are even more different than playing classical guitar', replied Adrian.

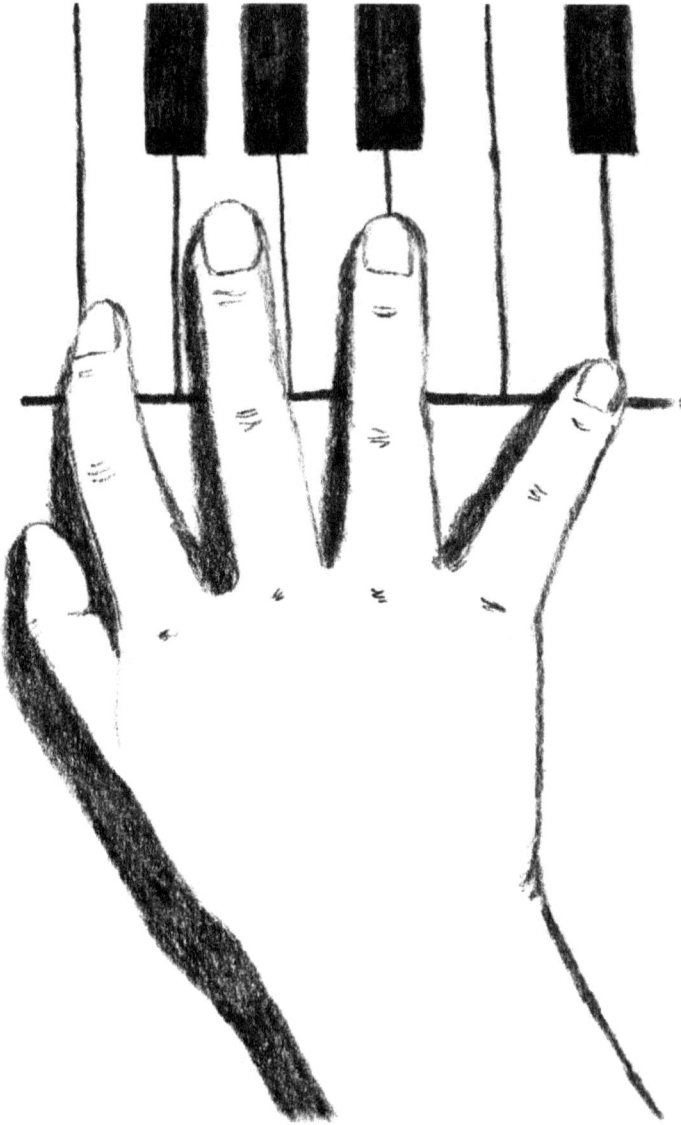

'Huh...well, I guess I can start with the basics for rock music and such. I'm not that much into classical music just yet.'

'Well then, that should be easy to understand, but what you must understand as well is that this isn't an overnight thing. You must keep at it.'

'Yeah, yeah, I know the drill by now'.

After finally arriving home and eating lunch, Adrian and Steven began the learning process immediately since Adrian also had athletics practice in the afternoon.

'Right, so before we begin, what questions do you have?', asked Adrian.

'You said it's not an overnight thing...so how long will it take me to learn this thing?'

'Well, it all depends on how fast a learner you are' said Adrian, with an innocent smirk on his face. 'However, you need to be wary of the fact that your fingers will hurt a lot in the beginning, and you might feel like your progress is a bit slow'.

'That or I'll learn to work through the pain', replied Steven.

'Anyhow, let's begin. Coach Jefferson really hates it if we are late.'

'Coach Jefferson also hates it when you breathe next to her. Or when you smile too much because she thinks you're not focused. Or when you tell her you're in pain. Or when you don't tell her you're in pain. Or…'

Steven went on for about two more minutes, to Adrian's amusement and silent agreement to everything he was ranting about. Truthfully, coach Jefferson was a ruthless athletics coach who demanded discipline and punctuality from each of her athletes. And while Adrian was a calm person, he often fantasized about putting her through the same torment she put him through at times.

'Anyhow, you know the notes and how they're called?', asked Adrian

'Yeah, the whole C, D, E, F, G, A, B, C thing, right?', said Steven.

'Yeah, that's the most basic of scales called the C major scale. What you need to understand first are the main components of a guitar. So, from top to bottom, you have the headstock, or head, which contains the tuning knobs or keys and string posts.'

'The knobs are those little key things that help you...do something with the strings?' asked Steven.

'Yeah, they help you tune each string so that it has a certain pitch when you play it'.

'The pitch refers to a note?' asked Steven once again.

'Yeah. The pitch is used to refer to how high you perceive the note. The higher the pitch, the higher the note actually is. The standard tuning for a guitar is E-A-D-G-B-E, from the thickest string to the thinnest, or lowest to highest sounding, if you will. If you want to be specific, it's E2-A3-D3-G3-B3-

E4. You'll find plenty of tuners online, which you can use to tune them.'

'But how will I know if my string needs to be tuned higher or lower?'

'Trial and error at first. And once your ear gets used to music, you'll be able to notice if a string is out of tune', said Adrian.

'Huh...mind waiting a few minutes?' asked Steven.

'Sure. What do you want to do?'

'I think I should write this down somewhere so that I don't forget it'.

Steven went on his computer and downloaded an image of a guitar and then added the names for each component mentioned earlier:

'So, what's next?', asked Steven once he was done.

'Next, we have the nut, this white piece of material here. Afterwards, we have the fretboard, where all the magic happens. Each guitar has a different number of frets. Yours in particular has 20'.

'So, what are these frets? What purpose do they serve?' asked Steven.

'Well, depending on where you place your fingers, the notes you are going to play will be different. Each and every fret is separated from the next one by what is known as a half-step or semitone. A half-step is the smallest tonal distance between two notes. Think of it like the equivalent to a meter or a millimeter for distance measuring.'

'Huh...let me write this down on my image.'

Steven then added the new components to his image:

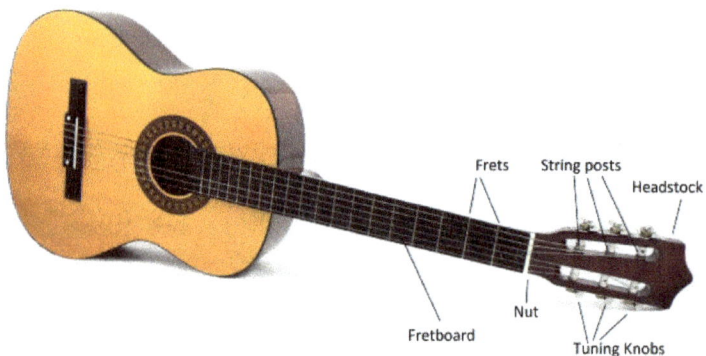

'Do you have any questions?', asked Adrian.

'Yeah, with regards to notes. There are like seven different notes, and I know that they repeat themselves because of that whole octave shtick. But

I am at a loss as to how the whole semitone thing plays into this.'

'It's like this', replied Adrian. 'Let's take the thin or high E string for example. If you play it open, without pressing any fret, you'll get an E note. And if you play it on the 12th fret, you'll also get an E note, but an octave higher. Octaves are the places where you encounter the same note, but with a higher or lower pitch. Between the open string and 12th fret are a total of 12 different notes, each separated from the next by one semitone. Everything clear up until now?'

'Yes, go on', said Steven.

'Right, so the notes between that low and high E notes are E, F, F♯, G, G♯, A, A♯, B, C, C♯, D, D♯ and finally E again. That symbol there is called a sharp'.

'What does ♯ mean? What does it do to a note?'

'A very good question that. Whenever you see a ♯ next to a note, it means that you should play it a half-step higher than the base note. So, F♯ means that you must play an F note, but a half-step higher. Similarly, whenever you see the little ♭ thingy, called a flat, it means that you play it a semitone or half-step lower'.

'So I'm guessing half-step and semitone have the same meaning?'

'That is correct. Just remember that a half-step higher means a fret higher and a half-step lower means a fret lower', answered Adrian.

'Ah, that makes it clearer. But how come there are no E♯ and B♯ then?', asked Steven.

'They do exist, in a sense. You might see them used in certain key signatures later. Just remember that E♯ is actually F and B♯ is actually C. And another thing that you'll notice in time is that certain notes have two names but sound the same.'

'So how do I figure out this equivalency?', asked Steven.

'Huh, how should I put this...ah, I got it. Whenever you see a sharp note, its flat equivalent is the note above it in the musical alphabet, with a flat sign of course. In other words, F♯ will sound the same as G♭. And before you ask, F♭ translates to E and C♭ translates to B. These are called enharmonic notes by the way.'

'So how do I know which notation to use again?', asked Steven.

'That will become clearer when you learn to read sheet music and understand key signatures. Just accustom yourself to how notes sound and we'll get to these concepts when the time is right. Anyhow, let's get back to the guitar. Under the fretboard we have the sound hole, which is where the sound goes and is amplified when you play a string. The part of the guitar that contains the sound hole and onto which the fretboard is attached is known as the body and the area where the string starts, so to speak, is known as the bridge. There are more components which don't really have that much importance in your playing.'

'Ugh...I'm starting to get a case of Too Much Info. Let me notate these components.'

Steven then added the remaining components to his image:

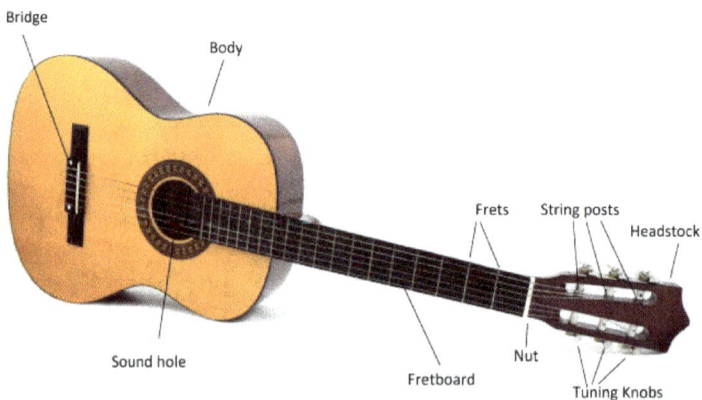

Adrian then looked at the clock and noticed that it was time for him to get ready for athletics practice.

'Right, I have to go get ready. What I think you should do is let all this info sink in and afterwards go look up an online guitar tuner and try to see if your guitar is out of tune. If it is, try to tune it. Then, start playing notes on different strings. You'll see that some of the notes can be found on more than one string. For example, if you play the B string on the 5th fret, you'll notice that if your guitar is tuned correctly, it should sound the same as an open thin E string.'

Steven had a look of despair on his face that seemed to scream 'What have I gotten myself into...'.

'Yeah, I'll be sure to do all of that, but for right now, I need a break or 10. You go have fun at your athletics practice.'

'Sure, let's call it fun', replied Adrian with a defeated voice. 'Also, when I get back, I will teach you how to replace your strings. Don't attempt to change them by yourself just yet.'

The ladder which Steven had to climb was much bigger than he anticipated, but for some reason, the challenge excited him quite a lot.

Chapter 3 - Steven Milner reads music

'Hey Adrian, is there an easier way to remember which notes go where on this thing?'

Steven had been busy playing notes on each string. Tuning his guitar turned out to be easier than he anticipated, even though he still felt he really had no idea what he was doing.

Adrian, busy doing some math homework, which Steven managed to do just before practicing so he would have time and not have to face some nagging from his parents, answered with a somewhat bored voice:

'Are you expecting a different answer than lots of practice?'

'Well, yeah. Can't you like embed them in my brain somehow?', asked Steven.

'Not without mom and dad having to answer some very interesting questions and us having to find the answers for them. But I do have something that may be of help. Let me just figure out where it was.'

Adrian browsed through his computer for a bit and then printed out an image, which looked like this:

'Huh, this is cool. If I understand this correctly, it stops at the 12th fret because notes repeat themselves from the 12th fret and beyond.'

'Yes, that is correct. Now let me finish this homework', replied Adrian.

'You know you could always copy mine, it's the same.'

'Yeah, not with mom and dad being aware that we do that quite a lot and then asking us questions about how we solved some things and us having about as much creativity as someone using the I-V-vi-IV progression in a song.'

'I have no idea what that is'

'Some say it's the reason people say all songs sound the same. Now let me finish this.'

'Can we learn something new on the guitar afterwards?'

'Sure', said Adrian.

After about half an hour, which Steven spent throwing a ping-pong ball at a wall, Adrian was done with his homework. Steven then sat down, ready to learn something new.

'Right-o then. Today, we are going to learn how to read music', said Adrian.

Steven almost fell off his chair:

'Learning to do…what now?' asked Steven.

'I mean, how did you think you can learn to play songs on this thing?'

Steven opened his mouth to reply but rapidly closed it since he had no idea what to answer. After a few more seconds of thinking, he finally answered:

'I don't know, I just thought, you know, you just kinda, just do it, you know?'

The bemused look on Adrian's face was the only answer Steven got to this.

'Anyhow, music can be represented in two ways: sheet music and tabs. We're going to go through both, though tabs will come in handier when you're only interested in guitar playing. Even though me saying that goes against some recommendations'

'Wait, people recommend not learning to read music?' asked Steven with a hopeful voice.

'No, just tabs. Don't ask me why, though. I just saw some videos titled this way and decided not to watch them at all. Sheet music is fine, of course, but tabs make things much easier for guitarists. I guess people need to get those clicks somehow…'

Adrian then started looking through his music notes. Steven was amazed at how organized everything was. He always noticed his brother was a tidy person, but never realized just how organized everything was in Adrian's world.

After a while, Adrian finally found what he was looking for.

'Now this is something I created to make things easier for me when I kept forgetting what each component meant'

Adrian then gave Steven the following image:

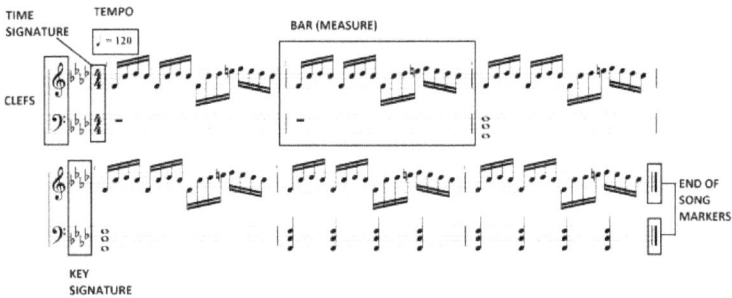

After glancing at the picture for a few seconds, Steven asked:

'Hey, I know what these are, you use them all the time when playing piano. You mean to tell me you still somehow manage to forget what they mean?'

'Yeah, music teachers sometimes, or rather usually, make us learn them by memorizing them rather than actually explaining them. And when I was little, I didn't really care that much, but it started to frustrate me a little bit'

'Oh, I see. I take it those little circle things are notes then?' asked Steven.

'Yeah, those are notes. The area on which they are drawn is called a musical staff. This piece, being a piano example and all, has two staffs. The one on the top is usually used to represent the main melody line of the song. The notes represented there are higher in pitch.'

'And the one on the bottom contains the lower pitch notes?'

'Yeah, they go by the name of bass notes the lower ones. And as you can see, each of these staffs has that weird symbol at the start, called a clef. Staffs used for higher notes use the G clef while the bass notes staff uses the F clef.'

'The who in the what now?' asked Steven.

'Ah, this one is interesting. They are named like this because, if you look closely, they sort of start on a certain line of the staff. For the G clef, you'll notice in a bit that it starts on the same line that the G note is represented on and the F clef starts on the same line the F note is represented on.'

'If you say so. But since we're on the subject, how do I know which note goes where?'

'I was just getting to that. So, for staffs using the G clef, the notes on the lines are E, G, B, D and F while the notes from the spaces between the lines are F, A, C and E. You can't have two different notes in the same space or on the same line.'

'But there are so many notes from what I hear you play. Where do they go?', asked Steven with an ever-increasing curiosity in his voice.

'You can use helper lines, like in the C major scale examples under this one.'

Steven looked a bit lower on the page and encountered two separate staffs:

'So, I just use those little line thingies to add notes outside the staff?', asked Steven.

'Indeed. There will be some notes which require you to add more than one line. You'll have to go through a lot of music sheets in order to be able to recognize them easily though. I have quite a few lying around if you feel like it.'

'I'll cross that bridge when I meet it. However, how do I know what C is played for the first example?'

'That is known as the middle C. On a guitar, its equivalent is located on the A string, 3rd fret.'

Steven played the note indicated by Adrian and then asked his brother to play it on the piano:

'Wow, something is out of tune here. Why does my note sound so lower than on the piano?'

'Yeah, I did some research in that direction myself. It happens with other instruments as well. Guitar notes sound an octave lower than how they're written on a music sheet', replied Adrian.

'It's kind of weird, though. I mean, wouldn't it be easier just to use two staffs?' asked Steven.

'Not when attempting to learn a fast-paced solo, it's not. Imagine having to move your eyes from one staff to another for the same melodic line. Quite the task that. Like I said, guitars aren't the only instruments that are like this. There's a bunch of other ones that sound an octave lower or higher than the actual note on the sheet'.

'Fair enough. What about the tempo area? It just shows a note equals a number.'

'That is actually read as quarter note equals 120 BPM. It's strongly related to the time signature as well', said Adrian.

'Quarter note like the...coin?' asked Steven.

'No, quarter note as in it lasts one beat in a time signature which measures the number of beats in quarter notes.'

Steven contemplated walking out, taking a plane to a distant tropical island, and never touching a guitar again.

'Ah, the faces you make when you are utterly confused are funny. I am assuming you are utterly confused, right?' asked Adrian calmly.

Steven nodded.

'Let's take it one step at a time. There are a number of different note lengths, and they are all closely related to one another. The more commonly used are whole notes, half notes, quarter notes, eighth notes, sixteenth notes and thirty-second notes. A whole note is the equivalent of two half notes. A half-note is the equivalent of two quarter notes, and so on. Everything clear up until now?'

Steven once again nodded.

'Good. Now, the next thing we need to understand is how many beats each note lasts. Usually, in rock music, the tempo of the song is measured by using the quarter note as the measuring note. This results in the following, um, truths with regards to note lengths. A whole note lasts four beats, a half-note lasts two beats, a quarter note lasts one beat, an eighth note lasts half a beat and so on. Here's a visual representation of each type of note length.'

Adrian then gave Steven the following image:

'Huh, at least I no longer feel like you're speaking bat. But looking at the whole sheet music thing, you also mention measures there. How do I know how many notes can go into this measure thingy?', asked Steven with a slightly less anxious tone.

'That boils down to the time signature. Do you see those two numbers at the beginning of the song? The one on the bottom tells you what note length represents one beat of a measure, and the one on the top tells you how many beats go in a measure', explained Adrian.

'So, for our song example, that time signature would be something like four quarter notes per measure?'

'That's exactly right', said Adrian.

'Oh. That's nice. So, for each of these measures or bars, when we have notes in them, we need to have, like, the equivalent of four beats, right? So, anything from a whole note to...' - Steven thought for a bit - '32 32nd notes?' asked Steven with a much more cheerful voice.

'Now you're getting it', replied Adrian.

'But I want to know something. What if I don't have to have notes for each possible beat? Is that something that can be accomplished?' asked Steven.

'It can be done by using rests', said Adrian, looking through his papers for the following image:

'Oh, yes, they were actually in our example as well on the bass staff thingy. Now, what about this tempo thing? You say it's measured in something called BPM. What in the name of sheet music is a BPM?', asked Steven, who was finally able to see how music sheets work.

'BPM is an acronym for beats per minute. The easiest way to understand how this works is to think about what 60 BPM means in relation to time. If a song is written in 60 BPM, then that means that each minute contains a total of 60 beats. Which means that one beat lasts one second. In other words, a quarter note lasts one second, a half-note lasts two seconds and so on.'

Adrian drank a bit of water and then continued: 'You'll sometimes find music sheets that use some Italian words to designate the tempo, but you can find the equivalency online until you understand them. Also, there may be times when you might see BPM values in relation to other note lengths, but more on that if you encounter them.'

'So, do I have to mentally figure out all these numbers before playing?'

'No, there are online metronomes that can help you. I also have a physical one lying around here, which you can use.'

'I feel like I just learned a new language', said Steven. 'You also said something about tabs?'

'Yeah. Tabs are a bit easier to understand. Here's a basic example here.'

Adrian then searched for another image:

```
E | ----0---- |
B | ----1---- |
G | ----0---- |
D | ----2---- |
A | ----3---- |
E | --------- |
```

'Huh. This is slightly less foreign. I think so, anyway. Those numbers tell me...what exactly?', asked Steven.

'Those numbers tell you which fret you should be pressing on your guitar. Try positioning your hand on the fretboard. Since you're using your left hand on the fretboard, you'll want your index finger on the B string 1st fret, your middle finger on the D string 2nd fret, and your ring finger on the A string, 3rd fret.'

Steven took his guitar and attempted to imitate the shape he saw on the tab. He then strummed the strings and aside from some muffled notes, because he was too close to the frets, the C chord which he attempted to play sounded not that bad.

'Careful with your fingers. You want to be on the frets mentioned there, but remember to not put your fingers exactly on them. You'll want to have them next to the metal area, not directly on it. Like a bit towards the left of it, since you are using your left hand on the fretboard', said Adrian.

'I see. What exactly am I playing here, though?', asked Steven.

'That is a C major chord.'

'Ah...well, I suppose I believe you. One final question though. Do I always have to play as many notes at the same time?'

'No, you'll have tabs where you only have to play one note at a time. However, whenever you see two or more numbers in the same position on the tab, that means that you must play them at the same time. You'll see what I am referring to in time'

'Makes sense, I guess. Do the fretting hand fingers have any names, or are they just index, middle, ring, and pinky?' asked Steven.

'They do have names. I mean, sort of anyway. They have numbers. So, the index finger is finger number one, the middle finger is finger number two, the ring finger is finger number three, and the pinky is finger number four. Note that this only applies to your fretting hand; the playing hand fingers have different names.'

'Are those names important to know?', asked Steven.

'Not really, though you may encounter them in certain music sheets. I am certain it's best to tackle them only if you want to go in that direction.'

'Makes sense. But now I need a break. It's been quite a trip today. Wanna duel in epic console football games?'

'Well, we do have about half an hour until supper time, so let's use it wisely'.

'You are going to lay off on the cheap distraction moves?' asked Steven.

'No promises can be made, you know that.'

The boys enjoyed a few games and then ate their supper. Steven was feeling a bit overwhelmed by the whole guitar concept, but after taking a few moments, he realized that he had made quite some progress and he wasn't ready to give up, not yet anyway.

Chapter 4 – Intervals and chords

Steven woke up the next day after having the weirdest of dreams. He was a time signature, and the notes kept coming at him for no reason. He honestly felt grateful that the alarm woke him up when he did.

'It's times like these when I think math doesn't feel so bad...', Steven thought to himself. However, with that thought came the sudden realization that today was math test day, so he started getting ready for school.

The day went quite well, and Steven felt confident about his results on the test.

'How'd you do?', he asked Adrian.

Adrian didn't answer. He kept looking either at the ground or towards another group of students. Steven was intrigued by his brother's silence, so he tried looking in the same direction that Adrian was looking.

He noticed that there were some boys and girls there, and that's when things got even more interesting for him. He needed to investigate this further when the time was right. And what better time than now?

'I asked, how'd you do on the test?' tried Steven again.

'Oh...yeah, right, the test. I mean, I think I did well. It wasn't as hard as I had expected. Though that last equation gave me a bit of a headache', replied Adrian.

'Yeah, it seems it gave you a headache so big it also twisted your neck, making you stare at other people', said Steven, with his eyes squinted and his smirk ever-growing.

Adrian felt something was up and quickly regained his composure:

'You're looking too much into things that aren't there.'

'Things might not be there, sure. But the fact that a certain blonde, green-eyed girl was in that direction is pure coincidence? ' asked Steven, looking for any changes in his brother's demeanor.

Adrian did not budge a single inch:

'Yes.'

Steven was not ready to give up this battle just yet, but he decided to change tactics a bit:

'Let's say I believe you. What are we learning today on guitar?' Steven continued.

Adrian, who was a bit rattled by the fact he was almost caught in this trap by his brother, managed to relax and answered:

'We're going to talk about chords. You know, playing multiple notes at the same time basically. I'll also teach you a bit about different playing styles, intervals and how your fingers fit into all of this.'

After a relaxing lunch consisting of chicken wings and vegetables, Adrian and Steven sat down and started learning again.

'Okay then. Let's start by going through the possible ways of playing guitar. You may have seen me use a pick at times'

'That little plastic thing?' asked Steven.

'Yes. You will want to use that when playing solos or chords. Believe me when I say that when you play a rock song riff, you'll want that.'

'What's a riff?'

'It's a vague definition that refers to the rhythm parts of songs. A riff can consist of a series of notes or chords that repeat themselves as part of the rhythm guitar. Or rhythm instrument, because you may hear that term used for other instruments as well.'

'So, when do I play without this pick thingy?' asked Steven.

'Acoustic songs mostly. Think of Dust in the Wind, Stairway to Heaven, Road Trippin', Nothing Else Matters and the like. If you look at the tabs for these songs, you'll see that you will have to play notes at the same time, but since they are not on strings next to each other, you can't use a pick. This technique is called fingerpicking.'

'Ok, I think I get it. But how do I know which finger goes on which string when fingerpicking?' asked Steven.

'Ugh, this might be a tough one to explain. Let me think for a bit.'

Adrian picked up his guitar and positioned his fingerpicking hand, which was his right hand, next to the strings. Scratching his head for a bit, he finally came up with an explanation:

'So, it's like this. It all depends on the chord shape you're supposed to be playing, and we'll discuss them later, but the basic idea is the following. Your thumb should be located close to the lowest string required to play and is usually used on the E, A or D strings at the most. Your ring finger should be located as close to the highest string required and is usually used on the B or high E strings. Your index and middle fingers are used for any strings in between.'

'Ok...', said Steven with an unconvinced tone. 'So, I won't get to use my pinky to play strings at all?'

'I don't think I've seen any guitarists using their pinky, so no. Anyhow, let me draw you some examples for fingerpicking.'

Adrian then took a piece of paper and began drawing. After a few minutes, in which Steven observed what he was doing, he came up with some examples, the first one looking something like this:

```
E | ----- |
B | --1-- |
G | --2-- |
D | ----- |
A | --3-- |
E | ----- |
```

'How would you play this?' Adrian asked his brother.

'Huh...based on what you have said, I'd have to go with my thumb on the A string, my middle finger on the G string, and my ring finger on the B string'.

'Close enough. Theory suggests that you should use your thumb, index and middle fingers. I find it more comfortable this way, you can try them both. Now, what about this one?'

Steven then looked at the next example, which was a longer one:

```
E | ------------------------- |
B | --0-----------0---------- |
G | --------0-----------0---- |
D | ------0-----------0------ |
A | --0---------0------------ |
E | ------------------------- |
```

'Oh, what is that?', Steven asked, his eyes almost out of their orbit.

'This was actually a very useful example I came across on the good old Internet a while back.'

'Ok, so, based on your previous points, I should be using something like my thumb and middle fingers on the A and B strings, then my thumb and index fingers on the next two strings, then thumb, middle, thumb, middle.'

'Try and play it', Adrian said.

Steven then attempted to play it. It was a bit mechanical and all over the place, but after a few tries, he at least understood the gist of it.

Adrian then continued:

'My ring finger feels the need to pick up the work from my middle finger. In fact, to me, it feels more natural to use all four fingers for this, with the index picking up the work from the thumb on the D string and so on. How did it feel to you?'

'Ugh, I dunno. I feel like I can get used to my method. I didn't feel any difficulty with it', said Steven.

'If it feels good, then that's all that matters. Now, let's talk about intervals.'

Steven put his guitar away and was ready to listen.

'A music interval is the difference in pitch between two notes. Their name consists of a number and a quality. The three most common quality types are major, minor and perfect. You can also have augmented or diminished intervals, but we'll cross that bridge when we meet it. Also, music intervals can be either simple or compound.'

'What's the difference between the two?'

'Simple music intervals contain notes located in the same octave while compound intervals use notes located in two different octaves. Compound intervals are comprised of two simple music intervals.'

'Right, can we like start with the simpler ones then?', Steven asked.

'Sure. You have a total of eight different simple music intervals. The first one is called the prime; its quality is perfect, and it is basically the difference between a note and...itself.'

Steven was amused by this statement.

'Moving along, the next one in line is the second, which contains two pitches between the start and end notes. It can be either major, if the notes are located one step away from each other or minor if the notes are located a half-step away from each other. C-D is a major second, and E-F is a minor second, for example. Is everything clear?'

Steven nodded.

'The next one is the third, which contains a total of three pitches between the start and end notes. It can be major if notes one and two are separated by a step and notes two and three are also separated by a step. If either of those two sets of notes is separated by a half-step, the third is minor.'

'Must the distances always be step and half-step, or can they be interchanged?' asked Steven.

'They are interchangeable, yeah.'

'Hm, got any examples handy?'

'Yeah. So, C-E is a major third, what with C and D being separated by a whole step and D and E also being separated by a whole step. D-F is a minor third because E and F are separated by a half-step.'

'By that logic, E-G would also be a minor third?' asked Steven.

'That's correct, and you see the first two notes are separated by a half-step here. The next two intervals, which are perfect, are the fourth and the fifth. Any questions?'

'Yeah, why are some of these perfect while others aren't?' asked Steven.

'It has to do with something called consonance. Basically, perfect intervals are perfectly consonant, meaning they sound perfect to the human ear.'

'That's...kinda mundane. I'm guessing for fourths we would have C-F, D-G, etc., as examples and for fifths we can have C-G, D-A, etc., as examples?'

'Yes, you are correct. Also, a particularly interesting case of a fourth is F-B, which is also known as a tritone, and it sounds a bit sinister.'

'Huh, can you show me?' asked Steven.

'Sure, here it is. Try playing a C-F and then an F-B fourths.'

'Funky sound that. Is it ever used in songs?' asked Steven after playing them.

'Not that much. I've heard some old game soundtracks use them, though.'

'That's cool. So, we're like five intervals in. Judging by the naming conventions, I suspect the remaining three are the sixth, seventh and eighth?'

'Close, the last one is called an octave. Sixths and sevenths can be major or minor, while octaves are perfect by nature. C-A is an example of a major sixth, E-C is a minor sixth. C-B is a major seventh and D-C is a minor seventh.'

'Ok, I get it. But what does this have to do with chords?'

'Quite a lot, actually.'

'Meaning…', added Steven.

'The idea is that the most basic of chords, major, minor, augmented and diminished, are obtained by stacking thirds on top of each other. By stacking, I mean playing three notes, each separated by a different type of third.'

'Huh. So how does this stacking process work? How do I differentiate between those four chord types you just mentioned?'

'Major chords contain a major third and a minor third, stacked on top of each other. Minor chords contain a minor third and a major third stacked on top of each other. Augmented chords contain two major thirds stacked on top of each other, and finally, diminished chords contain two minor thirds stacked on top of each other. You will also encounter chords referred to as triads, since the minimum number of notes required to play a chord is 3.'

'So, in order to play a chord, all I have to do is play three notes?'

'Yes, that is correct. Although, as you'll soon learn, on a guitar, you usually play more than three notes.'

'I see.'

'Now, can you figure out all possible chord types if the starting note is C?', asked Adrian.

Steven nodded and then took a piece of paper and a pencil. After a few minutes, he said with a happy face:

'I think I got this. So, C major is C-E-G, C minor is C-Eb-G, C augmented is C-E-G#, and C diminished is C-Eb-Gb. Is that correct?'

'Yeah, it is. Good work there', said Adrian, very happy for his brother.

'So, how do I go about playing these chords?'

'Well, there's something called the CAGED system for that, but let's start with the basic shapes for all the major and minor chords. Once you get accustomed to those, you'll be able to figure out the shapes for augmented and diminished as well. But before we go on to chord shapes, we need to talk about your fingers again.'

'My fingers?' Steven asked, not even surprised anymore by what he was hearing.

'Yep. The ones from your fretting hand, to be exact. You remember from last time that they had a number associated to them, right? Your index finger is one, the middle finger is two, the ring finger is three, and the pinky finger is four. Everything clear?'

'I guess so. Where are we going with this?'

'Well, take a look at this image right here'.

Adrian then gave Steven the following image:

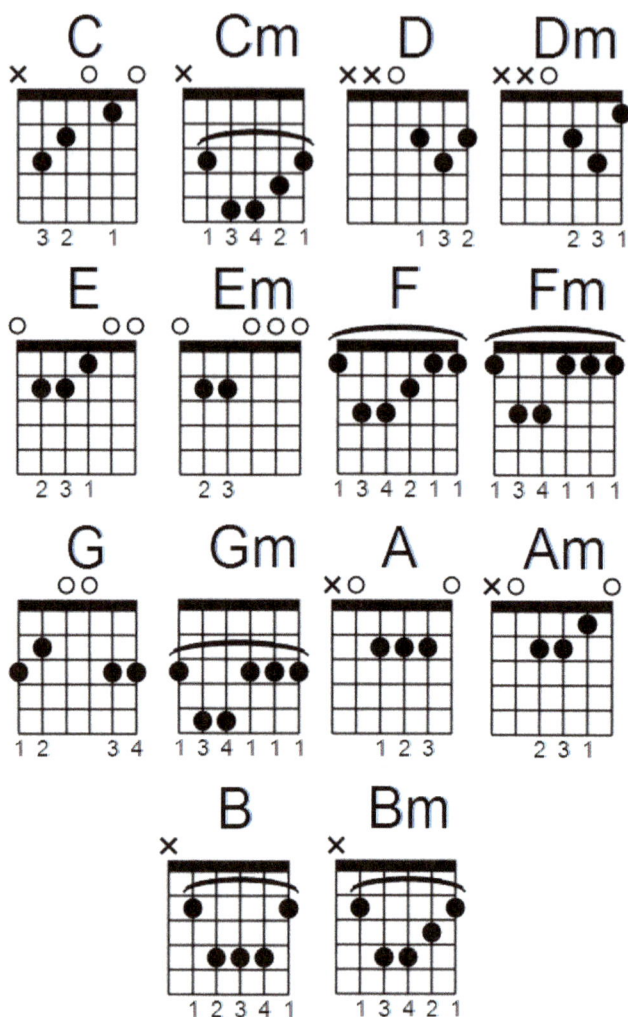

Steven glanced at the page, turned it around, and then glanced at it again.

'I think I got it. The numbers under the fretboard tell me what fingers to use on each string for each chord.

But what's with that parenthesis-like thingy on some of these chords?', asked Steven.

'That signifies that you have to use the finger as a barre, like this.'

Adrian then demonstrated what a barre looked like:

'Huh, that looks like the F chord from the chart'.

'It is in fact the F chord. Now, what you should do is practice moving between these chords so that you get accustomed to the basic shapes for them. Fm might be a bit difficult, so will B, but you'll get there. Don't worry if the chord changes make no sense. But should you find yourself in a time of trouble, try C-G-Am-F as a chord progression'

'Am stands for A minor, right? And when there's nothing next to the note name, I assume it's a major chord?' asked Steven.

'You assume correctly. Also, augmented chords are notated as aug, and diminished chords are notated as dim.'

'Huh. Ok then, I will have fun with this. Though I do want to ask, when are we going to get to the more fun stuff?'

'Well, the next step is for you to learn the concept of scales. Then we can talk about advanced chords and scales, the CAGED system, and then we can talk about the basics of songwriting.'

'That's dangerously close to a 'never' answer', Steven said with a disappointing voice.

'You know, it's funny. You didn't want to have anything to do with instruments before, and now, all of a sudden, you just can't get enough.'

'I guess it's more fun than I had originally anticipated.'

'You've been doing this for like a week. And you seem to understand things quite quickly, so you should be able to go through the remaining concepts quite fast. Don't worry, exercise and patience will pay off'

'Fair enough. By the way, I was thinking of naming my guitar.'

'That's nice and a bit weird. Then again, racing car drivers also name their cars, so…what name did you have in mind?'

'I was thinking Monica. And you can use that name when referring to it. I figured it's a name you'd like and one you'd like to say out loud more often.'

Adrian turned around without saying anything for a few seconds. Afterwards, he turned to his brother and said, in a calmer voice than usual: 'Adrian Bennett asked if we were up for a game of football today. I said yeah, it could be fun. I figured we'd run there, so we're already warmed up. And as a token of appreciation for your name choice, I am going to give you a 5-minute head start, which I highly suggest you use, because I'm about to beat all speed and time records for athletes my age when I run after you.'

Steven could hardly contain his laughter and giddiness after all of this. He could see himself progressing as a guitarist, and he was also glad he found an open area in Adrian's defense. Sure, it wasn't exactly console football, but he finally found a counterattack to his brother's distraction methods.

Chapter 5 - Steven Milner plays scales

Steven and Adrian rejoiced. The final day of school was upon them and that only meant one thing. Summer break was here, and aside from some athletics competitions which Adrian had to participate in, and their upcoming high school admittance exam, it finally meant a free schedule in which the boys could do what they wanted.

Steven had been practicing guitar for about two weeks now and had become pretty good at chord changes and reading tabs. He tried learning some of his favorite songs, though they proved to be far from easy. Steven usually resorted to using tabs for his songs since they were far easier to read than sheet music. As for the tempo, he finally started to have a better understanding and feel of when he was rushing or dragging during a song. And to his joy, no chairs had to be thrown at him to understand those concepts, even though playing the rhythm part at the actual speed of the song was hard at times.

Adrian felt a great sense of joy (with just a pinch of pride), seeing his brother evolve at a steady pace. And though Steven was still a bit sloppy in technique, he noticed that his brother showed no signs of quitting.

'So, we have like three months in which we can focus on guitar now, right?' Steven asked.

'Yeah. Three months and an extra week this time around, since we're supposed to start the new year of school on the 17th of September or something. Still want to better yourself at guitar, I see.'

'Yeah, now that I can actually play more than three chords without my fingers needing a doctor. Is it normal for them to hurt so hard?'

'Yeah, I also experienced this. And with steel strings, it is an even bigger pain as a beginner. Nylon strings, the ones used on classical guitars which I started on, are easier on the fingers. When I switched to an acoustic guitar, it wasn't that bad.'

'Huh, that's cool. I do hear the difference between your acoustic guitar and my classical one', said Steven.

'Yeah, classical guitar, as the name suggests, isn't really used in too many rock songs. Though Anastasia and The Stage do come to mind, now that I think about it.'

'On that note, what are we going to learn today?'

'Today you're going to learn about scales. And as you'll notice, this is another key part to be able to understand how songs are built and why the artist chooses the chords that they do.'

As the boys were walking home, their football friend Adrian Bennett arrived towards them, after running for a bit:

'Guys, want to play a celebratory 'school's over' football?'

'Yeah, but why'd you run? We have phones, you know', said Steven.

'Battery's out, guess that'll teach me to believe that 40% is enough', replied Adrian.

'I see. Yeah, sure, let's play some ball', said Steven.

The boys then informed their mother they'd be arriving a bit late for lunch and went off to enjoy some matches.

After an hour of intense playing, Steven and Adrian arrived home, took a shower and enjoyed their somewhat late lunch. The clock showed it was 2:30 PM when the boys finished.

'That was refreshing. Now, what about those scales?' an enthusiastic Steven asked.

Let's begin. The technical definition of a scale, which I know you love so much, is an ordered set of notes, all located within the same octave.'

'So basically, a bunch of notes located between a starting note and the same note but an octave higher or lower?'

'That's correct. There are a bunch of different scales out there, but the most common ones are major and minor scales. You may also find them under the name diatonic scales. These scales contain eight notes in total. 7 different ones and the eighth which it the first note, but an octave higher. They start and end on the same note, in different octaves.'

'Sounds simple enough, but how do I know what notes I play in between?'

'I believe there are some formulas for that', said Adrian.

'Why must you use forbidden school words during holidays?' asked Steven.

'Forbidden?' asked Adrian with genuine curiosity.

'I mean, come on, saying formula is dangerously close to referencing math or chemistry.'

'Or, you know, racing?'

'Oh yeah. Didn't think about that. You'd think we don't watch that with dad during race weekends.'

'Anyhow, major scales follow the following formula: W-W-H-W-W-W-H. W stands for whole step, H for half-step. Minor scales have the following formula: W-H-W-W-H-W-W'.

'Are those like tonal differences between the notes from the scale?'

'Yes. Now, can you figure out the C major scale notes?' asked Adrian.

Steven then picked up his guitar and attempted to figure out the notes. After a few tries, he finally got an idea of what he was doing:

```
E | ------------------------- |
B | ------------------0--1-- |
G | -------------0--2-------- |
D | -----0--2--3------------- |
A | --3--------------------- |
E | ------------------------- |
```

'So, the notes should be something like C, D, E, F, G, A, B and C. Is that right?'

'It is indeed correct. Now try the same but for A minor.'

Steven then repeated the process, starting on A and using the formula Adrian had mentioned earlier. After a few tries, he finally figured them out:

```
E | ------------------------- |
B | ------------------------- |
G | --------------------0--2-- |
D | -----------0--2--3-------- |
A | --0--2--3---------------- |
E | ------------------------- |
```

'So, the notes are A, B, C, D, E, F, G and A', said Steven.

'Yeah, those are the notes. Notice anything peculiar about these two scales, particularly with regards to the notes?'

Steven stopped for a moment to think, and then he realized what his brother was referring to.

'They seem to share the same notes but in a different order.'

'Yeah, nice catch. These two scales are relative to one another. Relative scales share the same notes, and as a result, they have the same key signature. You know, same sharps and flats.'

'So how do I figure out the relative of a scale?' asked Steven.

'It's simple. For a major scale, you look at the 6th note, which is the root note of the minor scale, and then play the notes from the major scale starting on that 6th note. For minor scales, it's the same thing, only in order to figure out the relative major scale for your minor scale, you look at the 3rd note from the minor scale, which is the root note for the major scale.'

'The root note is the first note of the scale, right?'

'Yeah. Each note of a scale has a degree associated to it, which sort of signifies its position and importance in the scale. In order, the note degrees are tonic, supertonic, mediant, subdominant,

dominant, submediant, leading and the tonic or root again.'

'Any particular things I should remember about these?' Steven asked, raising his left eyebrow.

'Well, the three most important degrees in a scale are the tonic, subdominant and dominant, which are notes one, four and five in major or minor scales. And they are important mostly because the chords formed on these notes can harmonize any note in the scale.'

Steven had a confused look on his face.

'Do you purposefully use words you know I have no idea what they mean just to spite me?' he then asked his brother.

'Oh yeah, definitely. It's immense fun'

Steven grumbled for a bit then Adrian continued.

'It's probably more down to the fact that I am accustomed to this to the point that it's quite embedded in my musical vocabulary. Anyhow, a song usually has two distinctive instrumental parts: the harmony and the melody.'

'So, what does each of those two things refer to?' asked Steven

'The harmony is the rhythmic part of the song, usually consisting of chords, while the melody is the lead instrumental part of the song, the one you usually hum or sing. The term 'to harmonize' refers to the idea of playing certain chords, on top of which the melody part sounds good', added Adrian.

'So, the idea is that if the rhythm consists of the chords formed on the tonic, subdominant and dominant thingy things, I can play any note as part of the melody and it will sound good?' a less confused Steven asked.

'Yeah, something like that. The idea is that the triads for these three chords contain all the notes from the scale, so you can play them as part of the melody quite well. Those three chords are called primary chords by the way, while the other ones are secondary chords.'

'So, you say those primary chords contain all the notes from the scale? Let me try to figure it out. For the C major scale, that would be C, F, and G. Let me try to play this out.'

Steven then fiddled around with the guitar a bit in order to figure out the triads for the C, F and G chords, and then came about with this tab:

```
E|------------------------|
B|-----------1-----3------|
G|-----0-----2-----4------|
D|-----2-----3-----5------|
A|-----3------------------|
E|------------------------|
```

'Oh, I see what you mean', added Steven. 'Basically, if someone were to play these chords, I can see that all the notes from the C major scale are present'.

'Yeah, that's the gist of it. You can do that for A minor as well as an exercise.'

Steven then fiddled around with the guitar some and then came up with the following triads:

```
E|-----0------------------|
B|-----1-----------0------|
G|-----2-----2-----0------|
D|-----------3-----2------|
A|-----------5------------|
E|------------------------|
```

'Huh, this makes sense. So, you say they're called primary chords because they contain all the notes from the scale, right?'

'Yeah. All the other ones are called secondary chords. If it helps, for major scales, the primary chords are all major chords, while for minor scales, the primary chords are all minor chords.'

'I do get all of this. How am I supposed to use scales? It seems a bit boring to play them just in one place like I just did'.

Adrian then started looking through his notes again.

'That's the neat thing, though, you do not play them in a single place. Here's how you can play the C major scale in various places. I'm going to show you how to play scales in two phases. The final forms of these scales will become a lot clearer when we discuss the CAGED system in a few chapters.'

'We're putting stuff in cages now? That's cool, I guess', Steven asked.

'Unsurprisingly, it has nothing to do with cages. Rather, it has something to do with the chords that form the name CAGED. But I'm going to have to ask you to be patient. Because the CAGED system sort of combines both chords and scales.'

'Fine. So, what about these scales?'

'Right. So, I'll show you how to play the C major scale. The first, let's say, phase is where we play the scale by itself. Then, we will add some extra notes from the C major scale as well. Look at these images.'

C major scale

Steven looked at the image, played the notes on the guitar, and said:

'So, that's the C major scale, right? '

'Yeah. The name on the image is really a big spoiler. And now, let's add some more notes around those we have already played.'

C major scale

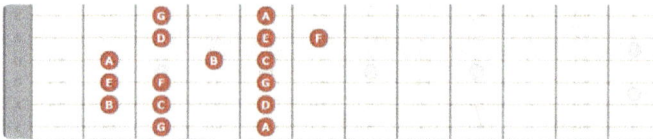

'Hm… I think I get it. You're basically adding notes from the C major scale, so you're not confined to three strings, right?'

'That would be the logic, yes'.

'That's really cool. Got any more of these?'

'Yeah. What you've just played is known as the A form of the C major scale, by the way. We'll talk about it once you get the hang of these scales, don't worry.'

'That's…not a bad idea.' said Steven, laughing a bit nervously as he realized the amount of knowledge still ahead of him.

'Ok. Here's some other ways in which you can play the C major scale. Again, two phases for each.'

C major scale

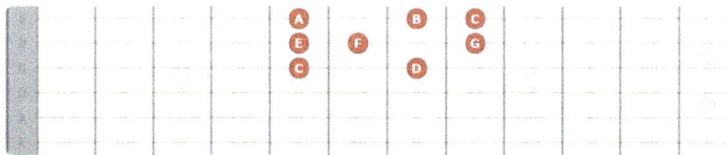

Steven then attempted to play these notes.

'Huh, so we're moving up the fretboard now, aren't we?'

'Yeah. You need to get accustomed to the fretboard at different positions. Let's add some notes now.'

C major scale

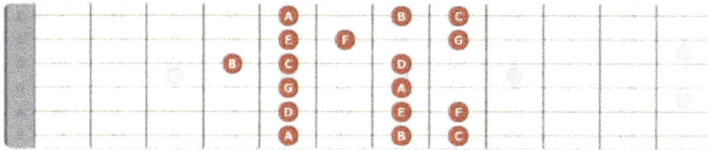

'This feels…complex. I think we should go through one more pattern only', Steven added.

'Sure thing. Here's a third way of playing this scale.'

C major scale

'Now, let's add some notes', Adrian added.

C major scale

'Huh, this should keep me busy for a while. Was there anything else you wanted to tell me?'

'Well, there are some concepts which will aid you in your scale learning, such as the circle of fifths, but I'm going to leave that for another day. What I want to teach you, though, is about natural, harmonic and melodic minor scales.'

'What are those?'

'The harmonic minor scale is obtained by sharpening the 7th note of the regular minor scale, which goes by the name of natural minor by the way. And the melodic minor scale is obtained by sharpening the 6th and 7th notes of the natural minor scale.'

'I see. So, for the A minor scale, the harmonic minor would contain the notes A, B, C, D, E, F, G♯ and A. And the melodic minor would contain the notes A, B, C, D, E, F♯, G♯ and A.', said Steven.

'Yeah, that is exactly right. When playing them in a descending order, theory states that you should play the notes in their regular form, meaning un-sharped, so to speak. I don't really remember why this is the case, but I just thought you should know.'

'Fair enough. I have a question, though. Since I've been messing around with chord changes, I can't seem to be able to figure out if the chords I'm playing make sense together. I don't know the technical term for that.'

'Hm, what I get from this is that you want to know if the chords are part of the same scale.'

'Yeah, that. I mean I can switch from C to G to A and such, but I don't really know what I'm doing.'

'Hm, this is more of a songwriting aspect, but let's discuss the basics. Each scale has seven different notes. In order to figure out what chords belong in a scale; you need to look at what triad is formed on each note. But knowing you, I think the following table showing what chords can be formed on each note of a major or minor scale'.

Adrian then looked through his files, and after a few seconds, he found what he was looking for:

	I	II	III	IV	V	VI	VII
major scale	M	m	m	M	M	m	dim
natural minor	m	dim	M	m	m	M	M
harmonic minor	m	dim	aug	m	M	M	dim
melodic minor	m	m	aug	M	M	dim	dim

Steven took a glance at the table his brother provided him. He then replied:

'I'm guessing M stands for major and m for minor. So basically, for the C major scale, we have like C major, D minor, E minor, F major, G major, A minor and B diminished as chords. And for the minor scales we have the other variations mentioned there, right?'

'Yes, that is correct. So now when you're switching between chords, you'll know if they're part of the same scale or not.'

'Sounds about right. I'm just going to go and have fun with this for now. But before I do that, can you show me some basic examples of how I can play the B diminished and C augmented chords?'

'Yeah, just give me a minute.'

Adrian then wrote down a tab version for the two chords:

```
E | - - - - - - - - 0 - - |
B | - - 3 - - - - - 1 - - |
G | - - 4 - - - - - 1 - - |
D | - - 3 - - - - - 2 - - |
A | - - 2 - - - - - 3 - - |
E | - - - - - - - - - - - |
```

'Huh, sort of thought it would be more complicated, but I can dig it.'

Steven felt more confident in his abilities after this day. The fact that he was now able to play chords from the same scale did help in this regard.

After playing around a bit more on the guitar, Steven and Adrian decided to use the time their parents were at work to play some uninterrupted console games. Their grandparents, who were taking care of them when the parents were at work, were a bit more lenient when it came to them spending time gaming.

Chapter 6 - Steven Milner learns the CAGED system

'Did you know that some people refer to certain chords as zombie chords?'

Steven was happy to have learned how to play in different scales. Well, at least the scales that contained the chords which he was able to play. He then started researching chords on his own, an adventure which yielded the question above.

'Really? And which chords might those be?', asked Adrian, who was busy obtaining enough experience points to level up in his mobile game.

'Some guy on the web mentioned that the chords in question are the ones that I keep messing around with.'

'Like the ones in the basic shapes or what?'

'Yeah, those. He suggests that if you want to have your own unique sound, you need to move away from them. You know, play them in different shapes. I don't really know how to go about that though.'

'It's easier than you think. Just let me finish this game here, and we'll get right to it.'

After a few minutes (which ended with a rather annoyed Adrian, who apparently could not beat the game), he and his brother started their new learning journey.

'If I could bash my way through that annoying game...anyhow, about those shapes. There's this thing called the CAGED system. The acronym comes from five movable chord shapes that we will use. They're basically the C, A, G, E and D chords, which you already know. And I'm going to show you how to use them to play chords in different shapes.'

'Oh, right, you mentioned that. Why are they called movable? Do they move?' asked Steven.

'Yeah, in the sense that you can move your hand up and down the fretboard in order to obtain a new chord.'

'I see. So, like, am I supposed to like play the C chord so to speak, but higher on the fretboard or what? Like use a barre chord like position?'

'That's exactly the case. Let's play the C chord using these five shapes.'

Adrian then showed Steven how the C chord looks in all the five shapes, in order:

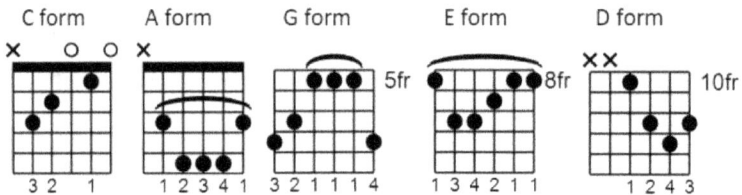

C form   A form   G form   E form   D form

Steven then attempted all the shapes. The C, A, E and D forms went around pretty well. When it came to the G form however:

'Do I really have to subjugate myself to the G form? From what unseen place did that shape appear from?'

'Yeah, I feel you on that one. I usually avoid it as much as possible. The A and E forms are pretty fun to use, though. The D form is also pretty nice sounding.'

'Hm, so does this system work for minor chords as well?'

'As a matter of fact, it does', said Adrian, who then gave his brother another chord chart:

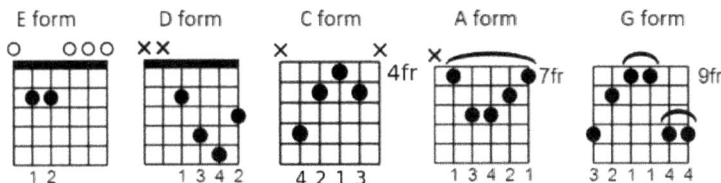

After attempting to play these chords (and letting out some very creative insults when playing the G form), Steven then said:

'Huh, they're in a bit of a different order, aren't they?'

'Yes, it's more of a convention than anything else. Mostly because Em is the first chord you can play in an open form. Though you could argue for Cm as well.'

'So does this CAGED thingy serve any other purpose other than learning chord shapes? It seems a bit bland', continued Steven.

'It's not food. It can't be bland. Boring, at most, if you truly want to describe it in such a manner.'

'I mean, it makes sense if you look at music as food for the ears.'

Adrian didn't have a comeback for this, other than his expression, which suggested he had lost hope in his brother's sanity.

'If this story were in video game format, the subtitles would read *grumble*. But going back to the subject, you can use the CAGED system to play scales as well. I think I have something here for the D major scale.'

'Adrian then browsed his computer in search for an elusive file.'

'Are you...narrating what I'm doing?'

'Yeah. Apparently, my mind gets very creative when I am on holiday', replied Steven.

'You should write a book then, or help Millie write this one… Here's the C form'

C major - C form

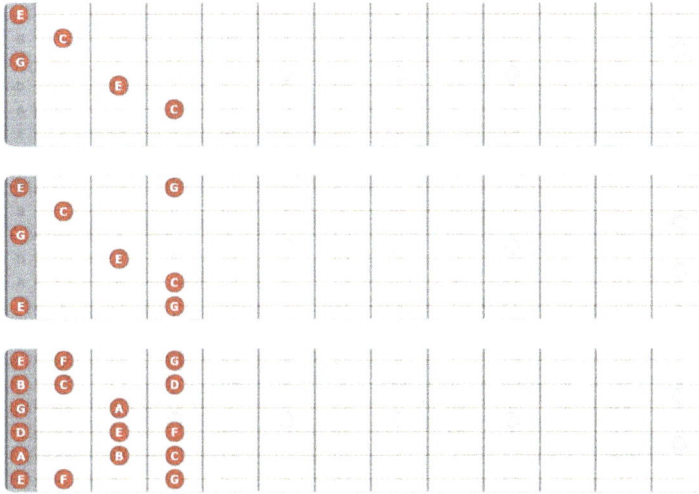

'What in music's name is going on there? Also, who's Millie? It sounds like you're glitching again or something', asked Steven.

'Well, we start from the chord, right? Then we add the notes from the chord around the shape. And then we add the remaining notes from the C major scale. Also, Millie is the guy writing this book about us.'

'Oh…that makes sense. Also, you're definitely glitching. You have one of these for the other forms?'

'Indeed, I do. Let's look at the A form:'

C major - A form

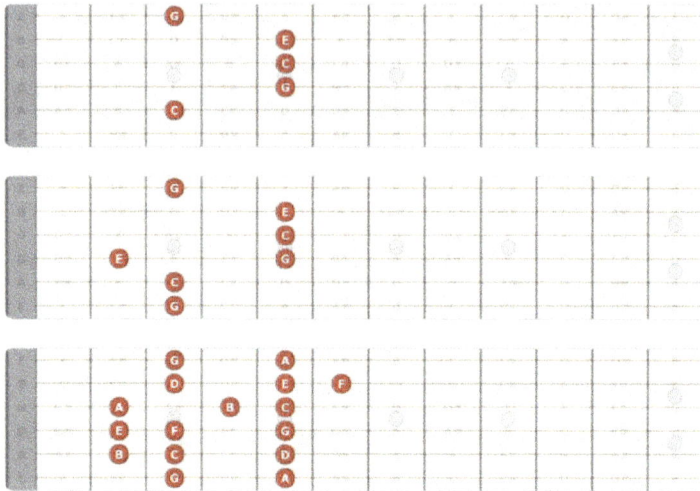

'Huh, this is actually easier than I thought. Everything is kind of related and linked to one-another.'

'Yes, and it will help you immensely now that you got that. Let's check out the G form.'

C major - G form

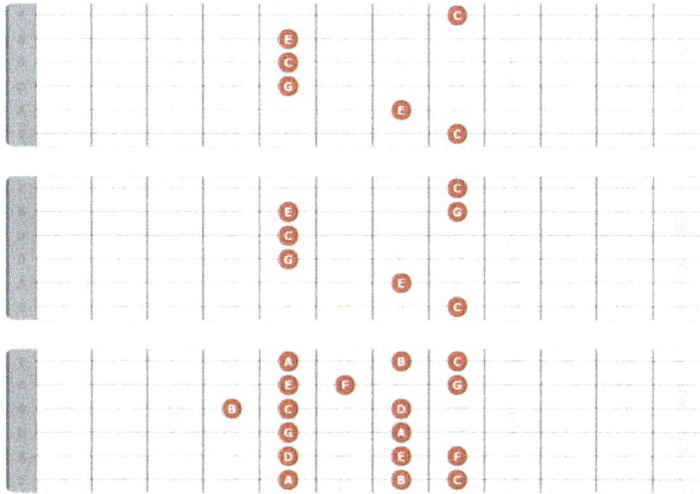

'This chord form is really annoying', said Steven.

'I know the feeling. I usually just skip the A and low E strings and only play the other notes.'

'And you're still able to sleep at night knowing you don't do something 100% by the book?'

'Yes. Well, most of the time. Other times, it's your annoying snores that keep me awake. Anyhow, I feel like playing some games, so let's get this over with and move on to the E form.'

C Major - E form

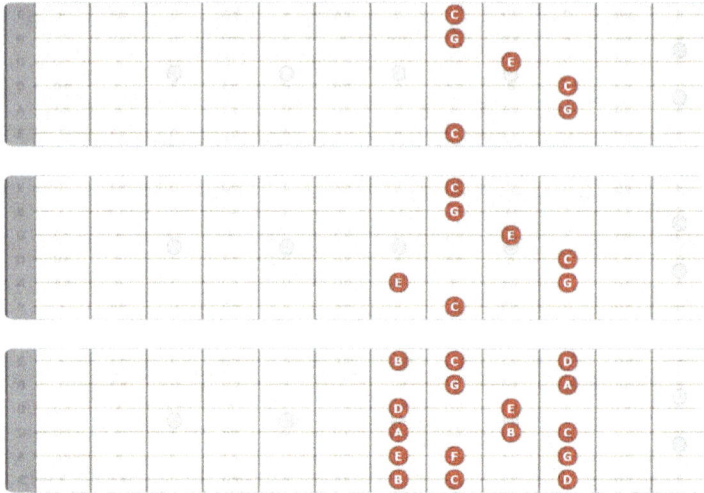

'I love how you only add a single note in that 2nd phase', noted Steven.

'Yeah, this form uses a lot the notes from the C major triad. Now, let's check out the D form', said Adrian.

C major - D form

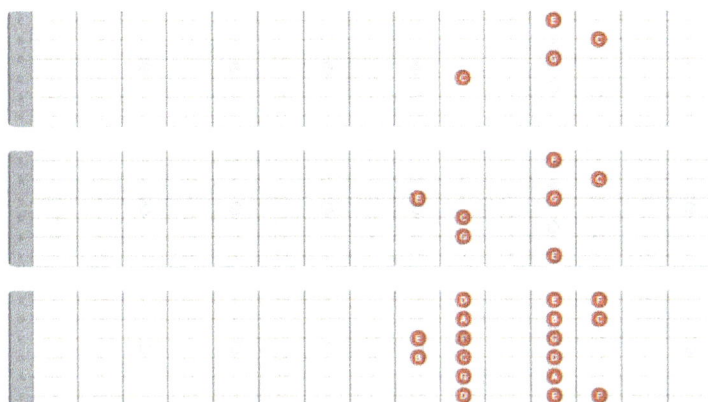

Steven then reviewed every form and noticed something interesting.

'These scale forms…it feels like I can kind of move between them. Like I can link the notes from one form to the notes from the next ones.'

'You're correct. It's actually a pretty useful technique to use when you want to create solos that span the entire fretboard.'

'That seems cool, actually.', said Steven. Then he added:

'So, you say I can actually play complex solos using these forms? They seem to be able to do the trick, but it seems hard.'

'It is at first, but you'll get used to them after some time spent practicing them.'

'That's like your default answer to anything, isn't it?'

'You've got amazing detective skills', replied Adrian with a sarcastic tone.

The boys were then informed that it was time for lunch. Afterwards, they decided to go ride their bikes in the park instead of gaming. Steven was feeling really good about his progress as of late. He wondered what lay next in his guitar adventure.

Chapter 7 - Steven Milner learns the circle of 5ths

Steven and Adrian were enjoying their summer break. The sun was shining, and their parents were busy with figuring out where to spend their summer holiday with their kids. Traditionally, they usually went to the seaside to enjoy the sun and the water.

The boys started going through what Steven had already learned on guitar, as a refresher course of sorts. Our long-haired boy was actually impressed by how much he has progressed over the course of a little over four weeks. Having discussed scales a while back, the next subject in Steven's adventure was about to be revealed today.

'So, about that 5-gear circle...'

'Circle of 5ths', Adrian corrected his brother.

'That, yeah. How does that work?'

'Well, it's a circle, kind of like a clock, but unlike the clock, you can go through it in both directions. By using this circle, you can figure out all the possible scales you can play and write songs in.'

'Huh, this sounds like a clock combined with that trigonometry circle thing dad told us about some time ago. But why is it called the circle of fifths?', Steven asked.

'Because, regardless of the direction you are moving in, you are moving in fifths. It's like this. When you're moving in a clockwise motion, you will be moving in rising fifths, meaning that you raise each note by a fifth. Each time you raise a note by a fifth, you are going to obtain a new major scale.'

Steven was more than confused.

'I'm not getting this. Where does it all begin, though? On which note?'

'It all begins on the C note. And if we start with the clockwise motion, the first note we encounter when we raise C by a fifth is G. And if we apply the same major scale formula but we start on G, we will get G, A, B, C, D, E, F# and G as notes'.

'I see', noted Steven

'Then, if we raise the G note by a fifth, we will get D. By applying the major scale formula again, but this time starting on the D note, we get D, E, F#, G, A, B, C# and D. And so on', added Adrian.

Steven seemed like he was finally getting the gist of things.

'I think I get it. So how long can we keep at this? How many scales can be formed by going in a clock-wise direction?'

'Well, since there are a total of seven different notes, that means that we can have a maximum of seven different sharps or flats in the key signature. So, by going in a clockwise direction, we can have a total of seven different scales. You'll notice that these scales make use of sharps in their key signature'.

'This key signature refers to the sharps or flats that appear in the scale notes, right?' Steven asked, trying to see how everything is related.

'Yes, that is correct. This is especially useful when you are playing songs written on sheet music. Unless the natural symbol is used, you have to play the sharpened note.'

'Now, about going in a counter-clockwise direction, I want to say that the key signatures will contain flats', said Steven.

'Your intuition is good on this one. When going in a counter-clockwise direction, you have to lower notes by a fifth and use flats. The first scale we encounter when we lower the C note by a fifth is F major, which contains the F, G, A, B♭, C, D, E and F notes. If we go another step, we get the B♭ major scale, which contains the B♭, C, D, E♭, F, G, A and B♭ notes. And so on.'

'This is a lot easier than I had anticipated. And that's a phrase I didn't imagine I'd be using this soon. Do you like have all this summarized in one picture like you seem to have everything?', Steven asked.

Adrian started looking through his guitar notes. He finally found his circle of 5ths chart:

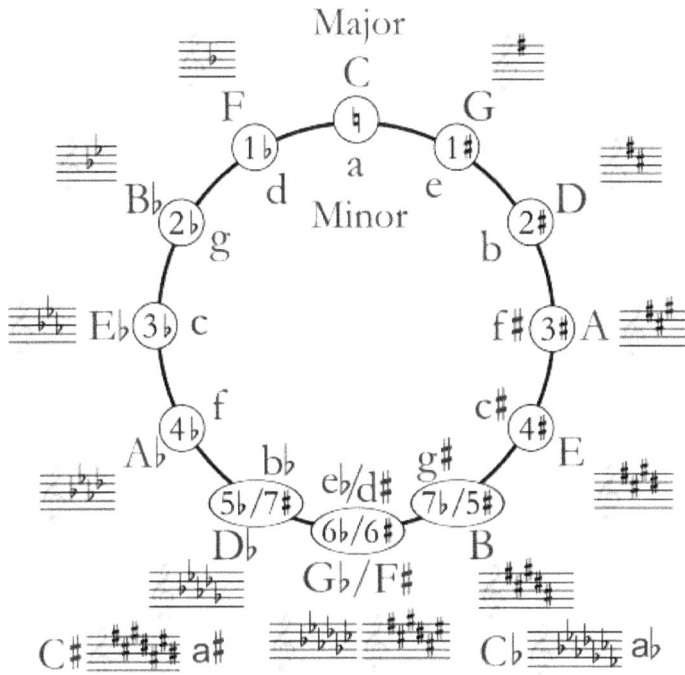

Steven started looking at the chart and then asked his brother:

'All the whole relative scale stuff and chord types on each note still apply in the same manner, right? Meaning that the relative minor is on the sixth note of the major scale, the chords are major, minor, minor, major, major, minor, diminished etc.'

'Yes, those rules are the same.'

'It's funny that some of these scales seem to overlap. I mean, what's the point of there being a C♭ scale when B is far easier to understand?'

'Eh, it is what it is. I'm guessing the idea was to have a full circle in both directions, even though the last three of each direction overlap with a scale from the other direction', replied Adrian.

The clock showed it was time for lunch, so the boys went to eat. Afterwards, since the weather was on their side, they decided to see who was up for some football and were glad to find that enough of their classmates wanted to play, so they decided to go and have some fun outside for once.

Chapter 8 - Steven Milner plays advanced chords

'You know, I've never actually seen you play guitar since we started this whole annoying teacher-misunderstood student gig.'

Steven was attempting to learn a simple song from top to bottom. But given the fact that the song in question alternated between single notes and some sort of chord-like sections, it was proving to be a more tedious task than he had anticipated.

'What do you mean? I've been playing guitar for years now. You've seen me play a lot of times', Adrian replied.

'Well, yeah, but I wasn't really paying attention up until now. And you seem to have been seemingly quiet on your instruments ever since summer break started.'

'Summer break has been going on for about a month, and I've played my guitar on a daily basis. And every time I do that, you mysteriously vanish or start playing video games in single player where you know I can't beat you'.

'Yeah, but...ah, never mind. Can you, like, play some random chords so I can get a better idea of how I can use the CAGED system and whatnot?'

'Yeah, ok, I'll indulge you. Pass me my guitar and my pick, if you will'.

Steven then provided his brother with his guitar and pick and Adrian started playing. Steven was listening very closely up until Adrian suddenly stopped, with an annoyed figure. His brother also noticed something was missing:

'I'm going to glue that thing to my hand...'

'Wait, where did your pick go?' Steven asked.

'Inside the guitar. Give me a minute.'

Adrian then began shaking his guitar to get his elusive pick out of the sound hole. Steven was bemused at the sight and at the annoyed grunts and noises his brother was making.

'Who knew you could lose your composure like this and show emotions? I always assumed you would do that only when talking about Monica.'

'Would-you-just-come-out-already?! Aha, finally!' a relieved Adrian shouted.

'Nice spectacle. I rate it a 10/10, and I would probably revisit the show on another day. On a side note, I loved the chords you were playing. What were they?' Steven asked.

'They were variations of regular chords. Let's call them intermediate and advanced chords. Mostly seventh and suspended chords, though. I find ninth and other variations to be either hard to play or not to my liking.'

'Wait, what? Do chords have legends about the 7th chord of a 7th chord now?' Steven asked.

'Not really. It's got something to do with the triads we discussed before.'

'The whole major, minor, augmented and diminished thing, right?'

'Yeah. You can obtain new chords in one of two ways. By altering the triad or by adding notes on top of said triad. Suspended chords are obtained by altering the second note of the triad while 7th and 9th and other such chords are obtained by adding notes on top of a triad. Everything clear?'

'I guess. By altering you mean adding a flat or a sharp or what?'

'No, you actually replace the middle note. You know how a major triad consists of a major third and a minor third? Well, another notation for such a triad is 1-3-5, because for any given note, if you play the 1st, 3rd, and 5th notes from the major scale formed on that note, you get the major triad. Do you understand what I am referring to?'

Steven nodded.

'Good. Now, you have two types of suspended chords: suspended second, or sus2, and suspended fourth, or sus4 chords. Sus2 chords are obtained by substituting the major third with a major second, giving us a 1-2-5 formula, if you will, for them, while sus4 chords are obtained by substituting the major third with a perfect fourth, thus giving us a 1-4-5 formula for these chords. Do you get what I am saying?'

Steven replied:

'I think so. From what I gather, I just replace the 3rd note of the major scale with either the 2nd note for sus2 chords or the 4th note for sus4 chords. So, if I want to play a Csus2 chord, the minimum notes required to play it on a guitar are C-D-G, while for Csus4, the notes are C-F-G. Is that correct?'

'That is indeed correct. Now you can play these chords in a number of different places on your guitar, based, of course, on the CAGED system. I find that the most impact for me is either in the A form or the D form.'

'Hm, let me give this a try. I want to see if I am able to play these without looking at a tab first.'

Steven picked up his guitar and played a C chord in the A form at first. He then stopped and thought for a few seconds about where the closest D note was located. He then played the following chord:

Csus2

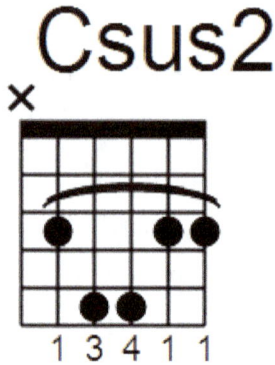

1 3 4 1 1

'Was that it? It felt like it was.' he then added.

'Yes, that's a Csus2 using the A form. Can you play it using a D form as well?'

Steven then played a C chord by using the D chord shape. After another few seconds in which he tried to figure out where the D note should be played, he came up with the following chord:

Csus2

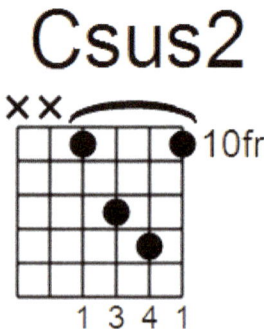

10fr

1 3 4 1

'This should be it, right?', an enthusiastic Steven asked.

'This is it, yes. I find that these two are the easiest to play and provide just enough of a mood change because the emphasis is on the altered note rather than on the root note. I mean, you can also use the other shapes as well. They look like this.'

Adrian then looked through his guitar-related files and came up with the remaining shapes for Csus2:

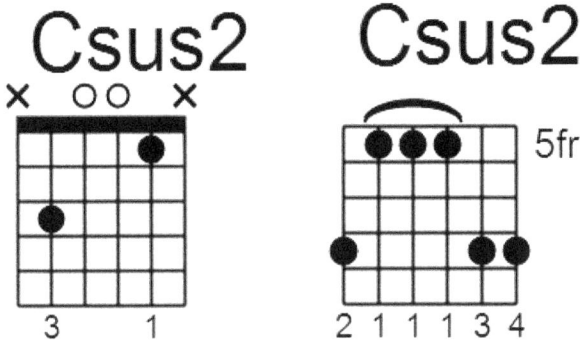

'So those are, in order, the C, G and E forms?', Steven asked.

'Yes. Now, shall we move on to sus4 chords?'

'Yeah, I think I actually know how to play the A and D shapes.'

Steven then played the following two chords:

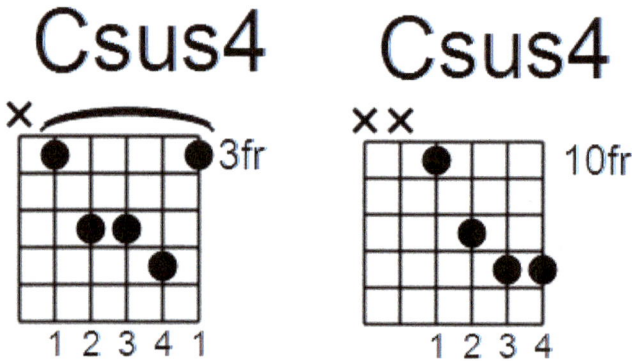

'Yes, that is the correct way to play these chords. When it comes to sus4 chords, I also find the E form to have a good vibe. Here are the rest of the shapes for Csus4.'

Adrian then provided the following chord shapes:

Csus4

Csus4

5fr

Csus4

8fr

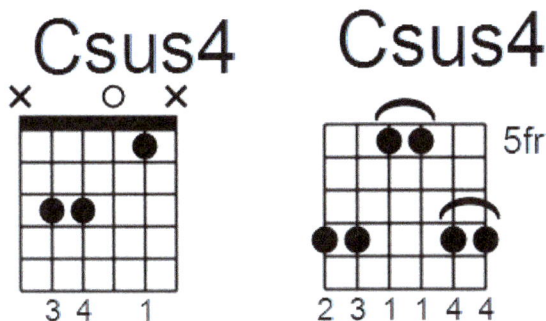

'Is that an actual normal-looking G-shape chord I see?' Steven asked.

'More or less, though it is easier to play, in a sense.'

'Hm, I like the sound of these suspended chords. They feel a bit tense though, as if they're saying I should follow with a certain chord afterwards.'

'In music terms, that is referred to as needing to be resolved. It's more of a music composition topic.'

'I see. So those seventh and ninth chords, do they function in a similar manner?'

'Not exactly. Those chords rely on you adding a note or several on top of a triad. For 7th chords, you are going to add a variation of the 7th note of a scale.'

'So, if I want to play a C 7th chord, I should add a B note?' Steven asked.

'That is the general rule, yes. You have five different types of seventh chords, though. The one you described is a major seventh chord and is notated as maj7 or in your case, Cmaj7. Basically, you take a major triad and add the 7th note on top of it. Always remember that the 7th note is in relation to the root note of the chord.'

'I see. So if I want to play 7th chords formed on the C note, I have to add variations of the B note, right? And if I want to play 7th chords formed on the D note, I must add variations of the C note and so on.'

'C# actually, given that the D major scale has the C# note, not the regular C note. Now, the next very common 7th chord is called the dominant 7th. It requires you to add a flattened 7th note on top of a major triad. You may also hear musicians refer to this as adding a minor 7th interval to the triad.'

'So, B♭ for C chords.', Steven said.

'Yes. The next two chords are somewhat related. The first is the minor 7th chord, which requires you to play a minor triad on top of which you add a flatted 7th note and the second one is called a minor 7th flat five chord, which requires you to add a flatted seventh note on top of a diminished triad.'

'And the last one is not called a diminished 7th chord because...'

'Because the diminished 7th chord requires you to play a double flatted 7th note on top of a diminished triad. A double flatted 7th note is the same as a natural 6th note, but because chromatic scales are a thing, you sometimes get these types of intervals. And if you were wondering, the interval between a note and a double flatted seventh note is called a diminished seventh interval, hence the name.'

'Huh, this seemed a bit more complicated in my head, at least theory-wise. How do you notate these chords though?'

'Dominant 7th chords are notated by using the seven digit next to the chord, C7 for example. Minor 7th chords are notated with the m7 notation, Cm7 for example, minor 7th flat five chords are notated as m7 ($\flat$5), Cm7 ($\flat$5) for example and diminished seventh chords I usually notate as dim7, though you may also see the degree sign instead of dim'.

'Hm, so still no love for augmented chords? Because judging by the logic behind these chords, I would assume that you could have augmented major 7th and augmented dominant 7th chords as well.'

'I never really thought of that until now. But yeah, you are correct, you could play these chords as well', Adrian replied.

Steven was very happy with this discovery.

'You know, it's funny how much sense all of this makes in reality. Our music teacher spends way too much time with theoretical stuff about music from forever ago', he then continued.

'Yes. The idea is that everything is related to everything. And while that's biologically questionable, in music, it's really a lifesaver. Now, here are the many ways in which you can play a maj7 chord. I chose the Dmaj7 chord for this example because I want to show you how to use a barre for the C form.'

Adrian then provided Steven with the following chord shapes:

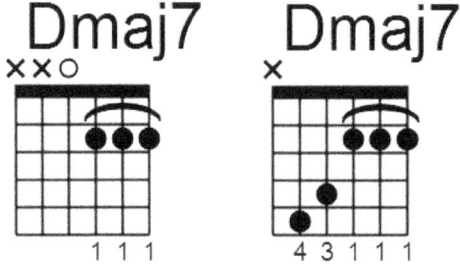

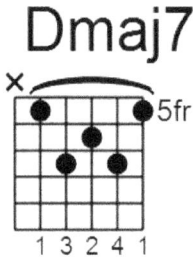

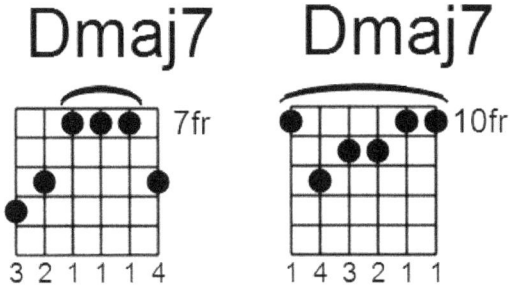

Dmaj7

× × ○

Dmaj7

×

1 1 1

4 3 1 1 1

Dmaj7

×

5fr

1 3 2 4 1

Dmaj7

7fr

Dmaj7

10fr

3 2 1 1 1 4

1 4 3 2 1 1

'Hm, are they in a different order than the usual CAGED one? The first example is of a D form if I am not mistaken.', said Steven.

'You are correct. I started on the D form since, you know, we were talking about the Dmaj7 chord. Let's now take a look at a C7 chord, in more shapes than one.'

Adrian then provided Steven with five ways to play the C7 chord:

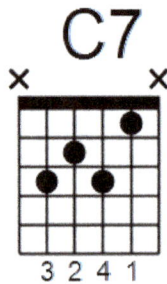

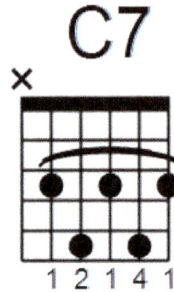

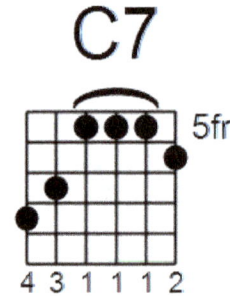

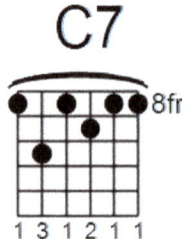

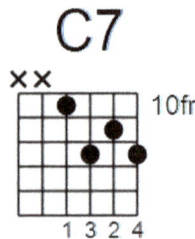

After attempting to play each chord, Steven was intrigued by something:

'This one has a dire need for me to play a chord after it. I just can't put my finger on which one it is. I want to say either F or G.'

'F is actually the chord you're looking for. It's because the C7 chord is formed on the 5th note of the F major scale, which is known as the dominant degree, if you remember. It's a very common occurrence to have dominant chords followed by root note chords in songs. It usually marks the ending of a section of a song.'

'I see. I'm guessing since it's so common, it's hard to use it without being called creatively lazy?' asked Steven.

'Eh, it depends. If you have a nice sounding melody on top of the chords, no one is going to care that much. Now, let's play some minor 7th chords.'

Adrian then provided Steven with another sheet of charts, this time for the Cm7 chord:

Cm7

2 1 3 1

1 3 1 2 1

Cm7

5fr

3 2 1 1   4

Cm7

8fr

1 3 1 1 1 1

Cm7

10fr

1 3 2 2

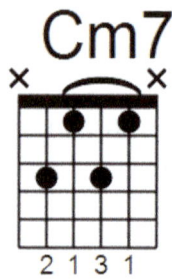

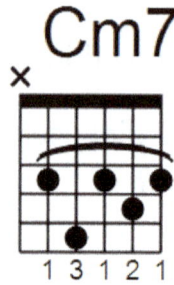

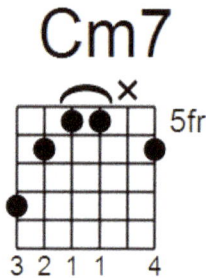

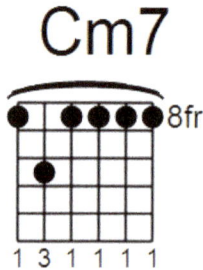

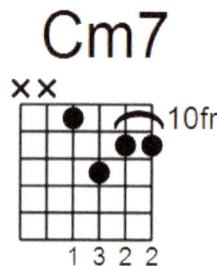

'Hm, I like the sound of this one quite a lot, especially in the A form', said Steven.

'Okay, then let's move on to the minor seventh flat five chords. I will suggest we stop here since these are more common. If you ever feel like looking into music composition, we'll look into them more then.

I actually like the idea of learning how to write songs, since aside from a few bits and pieces I don't know much about it', said Adrian.

'You mean you can't just pick the guitar and mutter some random chords on it in the hopes you accidentally write a hit?'

'There's always a possibility of that happening, but I assume knowing what you are doing beforehand might also be useful. Anyhow, here are those minor seventh flat five chords'.

He then provided Steven with another chord chart sheet:

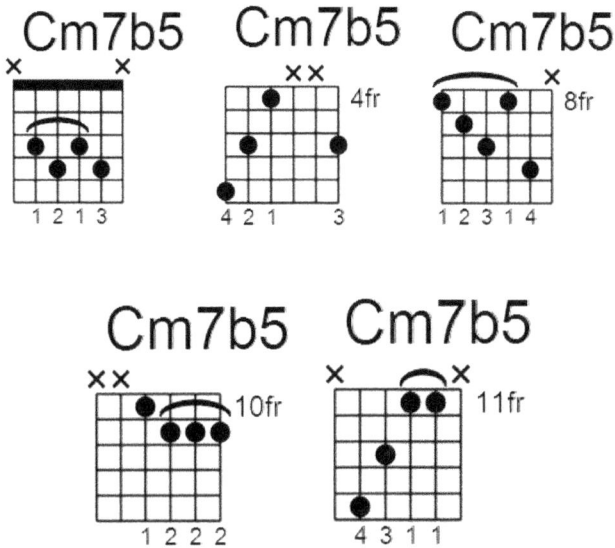

After a few somewhat unsuccessful tries, Steven gave in:

'Yeah, I think I'm going to stick to the A and D forms for this for like...forever.'

Adrian laughed, but he secretly agreed with his brother on the matter.

'Okay, I think that's enough material for me for now', continued Steven. 'But before I go into another despair arc with these, do those ninth chords function in the same way? I mean, how do I add the 9th note from an eight note scale to these triads?'

'Not exactly. First off, the idea of a ninth note refers to the second note of the scale, but an octave higher. So in the case of C major, it would be D, but in the next octave, after the higher C that ends the scale. Secondly, this is the place where chord formation actually splits into two possible directions.'

'Like in that cartoon with the dog and his weird gang?'

'Man, Millie really didn't research if he can use actual names in this, did he…though with copyright laws being the trainwrecks that they are…'

Steven had a confused look on his face. Adrian then continued:

'Anyway, back to chords. As you can see, we have added the seventh note on top of a triad. Should we have decided to add a different note, say the 6th note of a scale, we would have obtained another type of chord called the 6th chord. However, if we kept the original triad, say the major one, and then added the ninth note, we would have obtained a chord called an add9 chord.'

'This chord name actually makes sense', Steven noted.

'Yeah. A bit of a rarity now that I think about it'.

He then continued: 'Basically, when you add certain notes on top of a triad, you obtain added tone chords. The 7th chords are in fact added tone chords, but for notation's sake, all chords that add notes from the same octave on top of a triad are notated with the degree or number of the note that was added, e.g. 6th chords and 7th chords.'

'I'm guessing this changes for notes from different octaves?' asked Steven.

'Indeed, when we add notes from the next octave, we have two possibilities. The first one is the added tone chord one, in which you play a triad with a note, say the 9th note. And the second one is a bit more complex.'

'Why do I have the feeling it involves adding some extra notes in between?' Steven asked with a somewhat concerned look on his face.

'Because you've played enough video games to know that this is the answer, I guess. But yeah, in order to play a 9th chord, you actually have to add both the 7th and the 9th note, in accordance with the type of chord you want to play. Lucky for you, the 9th stays basically the same for all types. You variate the quality of the chord by using only the triad and the 7th note.'

'Yeah...lucky me. So how far does this go? How many of these chords can I play?', Steven asked.

'Well, you have 9th, 11th and 13th chords. So about that high. The 13th note is A for a C major scale, from a higher octave of course.'

'Well, this is going to give me nightmares. One more thing. If a triad is altered like when we play a suspended chord thingy, does it affect the 7th, or 9th or whatever chords as well?'

'It does indeed. Chords can get really complicated if you want them to, but it's not a necessity. It's more of a flex type of thing. Don't worry about anything higher than a 7th chord right now.'

'I love your enthusiasm. Oh, and in the spirit of a certain movie franchise, one last final thing. When can I use these chords? I mean, what purpose do they serve?'

'Adding variety to your chord progressions for starters. The idea is that there is a certain correspondence. Major chords in a scale can be replaced by major 7th chords, apart from the major chord on the dominant degree, the fifth one, which is replaced by a dominant 7th chord. Minor chords can be replaced by minor 7th chords and diminished chords can be replaced by minor 7th flat five chords.'

'Oh, I see. Well that should help me play a little less boring. And speaking of play, Adrian Bennett asked if we were up for some football. You in?'

'Sure. I need some fresh air. Let's go.'

Steven contemplated the new challenge. It seemed that every time he reached a new plateau, something even bigger came along to challenge him. It seemed hard, but for some time now he managed to turn the frustration of not knowing into a very useful energy that propelled him forward and helped him overcome any obstacle. And everything seemed to revolve around that high-school music contest his brother told him about.

Chapter 9 – Pentatonic scales, hammer-ons and pull-offs

'I'm beginning to think I hate chords...'

Steven had been busy in the last two weeks with some chord playing, but 7th chords had proven to be quite the challenge. Adrian had noticed that he had quite a nice variety in his progression though, and that put a smile on his face.

'Are you trying to get me to compliment you again?', asked Adrian, who was lazing in bed.

'No, I just think I need a little break from chords, that's all. Are there any types of scales I could look into?'

'There are, but that would imply me getting out of bed, and I don't feel like it.'

'What's the matter with you? You seem characteristically dull and lifeless, but you know...more than usual.'

Adrian replied with a very bored tone:

'Nothing. Just bored, I guess. Plus, it's like 100 degrees outside. Feel like lazing around a bit for once.'

After about half an hour, Adrian finally got out of bed.

'Right, you said something about some scales?'

'Yeah. I figured since I've gone through a lot of theory regarding the rhythm thingy of a song, we'd talk about the melody, since I'm guessing you usually play a melody by using single notes.'

'You can technically have two notes at a time as part of the melody, usually thirds. Metal bands do that a lot. Basically, you can use either regular major or minor scales or you can make use of pentatonic scales.'

'Penta-what's it now?', asked Steven.

'Pentatonic scales, which consist of five notes instead of the usual seven. They are based on the major and minor scales though.'

'So how do they work?'

'Well, major pentatonic scales are obtained by taking the first, second, third, fifth and sixth notes of the major scale and forming a scale with them. Minor pentatonic scales are obtained by taking the first, third, fourth, fifth and seventh notes of the minor scale and forming a scale with them.'

Steven then thought for a few second:

'So, if I want a C major pentatonic scale, that would imply that I would need to play the C, D, E, G and A notes right? And for A minor pentatonic, that would imply that I would need to play the A, C, D, E and G notes.'

'Yes, that is correct. These scales, particularly minor pentatonic scales, are extremely useful when you want to write solos for songs. They're especially used in rock music, though some guitarists like to improve them by adding extra notes, either from the original major or minor scale, or chromatic notes, meaning notes that are not normally part of the scale. Think F♯ or B♭ for the C major scale.'

'Hm, I see. That sounds interesting. Let me try playing the A minor pentatonic scale.'

Steven then grabbed his guitar and after a few tries, came up with the following musical sequence:

```
E | ---------------------- |
B | ---------------------- |
G | ---------------------- |
D | ----------------5--7-- |
A | --------5--7---------- |
E | --5--8---------------- |
```

'That's good. You can actually keep going till the high E string. Here, let me show you.'

Adrian then played the following musical sequence:

```
E | ------------------------------5--8--5-- |
B | --------------------------5--8---------- |
G | --------------------5--7---------------- |
D | -------------5--7----------------------- |
A | --------5--7---------------------------- |
E | --5--8---------------------------------- |
```

Steven noticed something peculiar about Adrian's playing style:

'Hey, is it just mc, or did you not pick all the notes with your right hand?'

Adrian was a bit confused but then realized what his brother was talking about:

'Right, I haven't told you about these techniques. What you saw me do goes by the name of hammer-on. It's a technique that allows you to add speed to your playing and also help you in tying notes together, which in music is called legato.'

'So, what you're saying is that I should just like, smash my finger on the fretboard so that it produces a note?'

'Yeah, something like that. Just make sure you don't rush to do the hammer-on. I remember when I first discovered this technique, I was so caught up in doing the hammer-on that I used to rush to do it, not allowing the original note to play for the required length.'

'Let's see if I get this. So, for the example that I just played, for the low E string, I would normally use my index and pinky fingers on the 5th and 8th frets. Using a hammer-on would imply that I should play the 5th fret note and then like smash my pinky on the 8th fret?'

'Yes, that is correct. You don't need to smash it like a hammer, though, just enough to get the sound out. Out of enthusiasm, you'll notice that the first times you do this, you may tend to overdo it, so to speak. By the way, before we move on, whenever you see tabs for sections that require hammer-ons, you'll see the letter h between the two notes.'

Steven then attempted to play the same sequence his brother played earlier, this time using hammer-ons as well. And at first, the hammer-ons felt really clunky and overdone, but after a few tries, he managed to play it perfectly. He even wrote the sequence down, with notations for hammer-ons as well:

```
E|------------------------------5h8--5--|
B|--------------------------5h8---------|
G|---------------------5h7--------------|
D|-------------5h7----------------------|
A|--------5h7---------------------------|
E|--5h8--------------------------------|
```

'Is there like a reverse technique for this? You know, like a hammer-on, but from a higher to a lower fret?' asked Steven.

'There is. It's called a pull-off, notated with the letter p. You will play the higher note first and then remove the finger from the higher fret. Make sure you also pick the string when pulling off. Here's an example, also in the key of A minor pentatonic.'

Adrian then played the following sequence:

```
E|--8p5---------------------------------|
B|--------8p5---------------------------|
G|-------------7p5----------------------|
D|-------------------7p5----------------|
A|-------------------------7p5----------|
E|-----------------------------8p5/8\5--|
```

Steven paid very close attention and noticed something interesting at the last notes:

'Huh, that was actually cool what you did there. Are those called slides, by any chance? Because I seem to hear that kind of sound in certain songs.'

'They are called slides, indeed. Slides are extremely useful when you want to switch between pentatonic scale patterns or registers, if you will. Actually, this is one of the reasons I want to start delving into music composition. I tend to get stuck in the same area of the guitar for too long.'

Steven didn't even attempt a snarky comment at the many new words he was learning. Adrian was mildly surprised at this:

'What, no witty comeback?'

'No, I admit defeat this time. Just get going and show me what you're talking about.'

'What I mean by patterns is this. The pentatonic scale, much like any other scale, can be played in multiple places. Unlike the major scales, though, you have only five different possible shapes. Let's start off with this one, which is located in the lower part of the fretboard.'

'I've been meaning to ask, to guitarists actually use that lower area in their solos? Most of the time it feels they are really high on the fretboard.', Steven asked.

'It's used, though not as much. This form however can also be transposed an octave higher, which means playing it 12 frets higher in the same shape'.

Adrian then showed his brother the following image:

A minor pentatonic - 1st form

'Seems simple enough. What's the next one like?', asked Steven after playing it.

Adrian then showed him the 2nd form:

A minor pentatonic - 2nd form

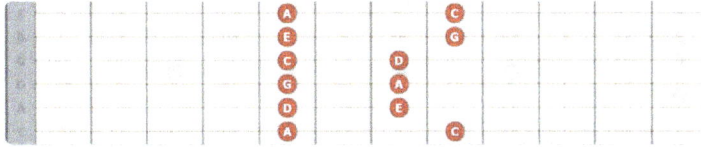

'Ah, this is the one we've been playing earlier, right?', asked Steven.

'Yeah, that's correct. Let's move on to the 3rd one.'

Adrian then showed him the following form:

A minor pentatonic - 3rd form

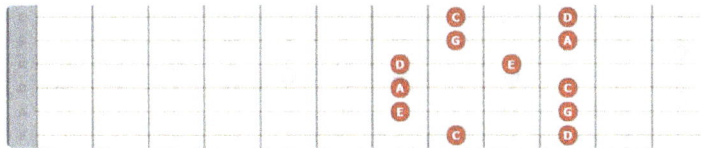

'Hm, this one feels a bit annoying. I don't know why, but I feel the need to play the F note instead of the E note on that G string'.

'I didn't have that problem as much, but I think it's because the previous two strings make use of that 10th fret and inertia kicks in'.

'Still summer break brother, come on, no physics stuff'.

'That's…um…anyway, here's the 4th one'.

A minor pentatonic - 4th form

'Ok, this one is definitely more annoying. Switching positions in the middle of the solo seems difficult. But I guess it comes with the trade.'

'It does. Wait till you see and learn about sweep picking using these patterns.'

'We…sweep guitar off their feet now or what?', asked Steven.

'Quite the contrary. Sweep picking is where the guitar somehow manages to become sentient, lays you down, and makes you cry a lot because of your incompetence at building speed. I may or may not be speaking from personal experience. Anyway, here's the final one':

A minor pentatonic - 5th form

'Hm...I see that the continuation from this one is basically the first one, 12 frets higher'.

'That's correct', said Adrian.

'I see. So, you said that slides help me move between these things, right?', asked Steven.

'Yes. The first thing I recommend is to accustom yourself to each pattern so as to build the muscle memory for your fingers. Afterwards, you can start sliding in between them'.

'Ugh, this seems complicated. You say this is an area in which you are lacking?'

'Yes, I'm not very creative when it comes to writing melodies. I tend to get stuck in the same pattern for way too long'.

'So, these patterns are for the A minor pentatonic. They can be used for other minor pentatonic scales as well, right? I only have to start on a different fret'.

'That would be correct.'

'So much to learn still.... Anyhow, how's your mood? Feeling better?'

'Yeah, but you're getting there'.

'And where is 'there' exactly?'

'I don't know. I never really know where we're going, just where we've been'.

'Lunch time?', asked Steven.

'Lunch time sounds good'.

The clock indeed showed that it was lunch time, so the boys were called by their parents, who were having some days off, in order to eat. Afterwards, they took their bikes and went for a ride with some friends. Adrian was feeling a bit better, while Steven was a bit concerned with the leap of faith required to learn pentatonic scales.

Chapter 10 – Power chords, economy and hybrid picking, and tapping

'Hammer-on, note, hammer-on, slide. Huh, this is actually sounding pretty good.'

Steven Milner had been busy with pentatonic scales. And while he was afraid to leave the A minor pentatonic behind for the time being, the melodies he was coming up with were starting to sound pretty good. Two and a half months into his guitar journey and his playing technique was correct most of the times, though he did feel he was still lacking in the speed department.

Adrian's mood was miles better than a few days ago and he was listening to what his brother was playing.

'You know, with a bit of work, you could actually make a solo out of that. Not the most versatile one maybe, but one that would certainly please the ear', Adrian said.

'That would be something, though I wouldn't know on top of which chord progression it would work. Something written in the key of A minor, I presume', Steven replied.

'That would be a good starting point. It has the potential to become something for a harder sounding song. You could write a chord progression using power chords.'

'Power chords? Like, do you need a power outlet for them?'

'No. Well, you need a power outlet for an amp but not for the chords themselves. Power chords are easily played, though. You need to take a root note, the note located a 5th above the root note and the first note an octave higher. They're notated by using the five digit as a result. You know, C5, G5 etc.'

Steven then attempted to play a C5 chord, which looks something like this:

```
E | - - - - - |
B | - - - - - |
G | - - 5 - - |
D | - - 5 - - |
A | - - 3 - - |
E | - - - - - |
```

'Only you would forget to teach me the simple stuff, I guess.'

'It was an honest mistake. I wanted to, but I forgot. Then I remembered, but you were busy with 7th chords. Anyhow, power chords are extremely useful when it comes to rock music. Most rhythm parts are written with such chords.'

'Yeah, it kind of feels like it', Steven said while playing other power chords. He then continued: 'But I've been playing close attention to songs as of late, and there are some in which there seem to be some of these power chords, but sort of muted. What's that about?'

'It's called palm-muting. It's designated with the letters P.M. on a guitar tab. And you obtain it by placing the outside of your playing hand on the strings, next to the bridge of the guitar.'

'That would be the lower area of the guitar where the strings actually sort of enter it, right?'

'Yes. You can obtain varying degrees of this effect, depending on how high or low you place the hand. Make sure you still have a bit of sound in there though.'

Steven then tried to obtain that effect. It was a bit hard to distinguish since he was attempting to reproduce it on a classical guitar.

'Hm, I'm assuming it sounds better on an electric guitar', he said.

'Yes. However, you may see it used on acoustic or classical guitars as well, so don't worry about it. It's fairly common when rock bands do acoustic covers of their heavier songs.'

'I see. Since we're on the subject, are there any other techniques worth learning from rock songs?'

'There are plenty. We could start with how you can use the guitar pick. By now, you have only been using what is known as alternate picking. The down-up motion you've been using from the start.'

'I mean, it's kind of obvious that you should be playing chords up and down if you want any sort of speed. Who wouldn't figure that out?'

Adrian didn't respond, instead, he started looking in a totally different direction.

'Wait, you mean to tell me you didn't use this alternate picking thing from the start?' Steven asked, with an amused tone.

'Let's just say I accidentally stepped into the shoes of someone named James. It also made want to yell 'Yeah!' a lot after some riffs. Quite cool.'

'So, what, you kept using a downward motion for every chord?'

'Yes. I then got accustomed to alternate picking as well', Adrian said.

'I see. Anyhow, I'm guessing this is the part where we talk about different ways in which you can use the pick.'

'Yes. One way in which you can do this is called economy picking. It's called that way because it helps you save energy by improving the alternate picking technique. It only works for groups of three notes. And with a bit of creativity, you can use it on any group containing an odd number of notes, but more often than not, it's used on groups of three notes.'

'So how does it work?'

'Let me show you. Pay close attention to my picking hand.'

Adrian then played the following musical section:

```
E | ------------------------------------5-7-8---|
B | ---------------------------5-6-8----------|
G | ---------------------5-7-5----------------|
D | ---------------5-7-5----------------------|
A | ---------5-7-5----------------------------|
E | ---5-7-8----------------------------------|
```

Steven then noted:

'So, let me see if I understand this. Your picking hand went down-up-down on the low E string and then down-up-down as well in the A string as well and so on.'

'Yes, that is the gist of it. You see why you need three notes?'

'Yeah, it makes sense. You need to end on a downstroke in order to continue to the next string. However, what happens when the melody is the other way? Like when you go from a higher string to a lower string?'

'You need to switch the order in which you pick the notes. So, if you go from the high E string to like B and so on, you go up-down-up, on the high E string then, up-down-up on the B string and so on. Something like this':

```
E|---8-7-5-------------------------------|
B|----------8-6-5------------------------|
G|---------------7-5-7-------------------|
D|--------------------7-5-7--------------|
A|-------------------------7-5-7---------|
E|------------------------------8-7-5---|
```

'Oh, I get it', said Steven after seeing his brother play it.

'Yes. I was a bit confused about this whole up-down thing, but for me, it finally worked when I understood that downward motions are towards my feet and upward motions are toward my head.'

'I always find it funny how some things feel more natural to me than to you.'

'What can I say? I have to have everything clear to the lowest level possible in my head sometimes. Anyhow, economy picking is useful if you want to take your speed to the next level. I haven't really gotten too accustomed to it just yet, but it's something I want to get better at.'

'I see. Any other techniques worth learning?'

'Well, there's also another type of picking called hybrid picking. It involves using both a pick and your fingers. I can't think of any songs that might use this, though.'

'It seems needlessly complicated. I mean, I think if I ever come across such a song, I might understand why it's useful, but until then...', Steven continued.

'Yeah, I didn't bother with it too much. What I did bother with is something called tapping.'

'Tapping?', Steven asked.

'Yes. It's done by using your playing hand and sounding a note on a fret by tapping said fret with one of your fingers, usually the index finger. Think of it as like a sort of hammer-on, but with your playing hand, rather than the hand you use on the fretboard. Something like this:'

```
        T               T               T
E|---17p10h14p10--17p10h14p10--17p10h14p10----|
B|--------------------------------------------|
G|--------------------------------------------|
D|--------------------------------------------|
A|--------------------------------------------|
E|--------------------------------------------|
```

Steven then attempted the tapping technique. It seemed simple enough for him.

'Okay, so just tapping a note is easy enough. I suspected there is more to this than meets the eye'.

'There is. But you have to listen to understand exactly what I am referring to. Check out the solo from One by Metallica and the intro from The Stage by Avenged Sevenfold.'

'Hm, I think I get what you are referring to. For something that starts off so simple, it seems to evolve into something completely stunning if done right'.

'It's quite the interesting technique because it allows for insane distances between notes. Something which is really easily done on a piano but quite difficult to obtain on a guitar. And after some further research, I've also learned of a thing called eight finger tapping. That's actually obtained by using both of your hands to tap notes. I didn't even want to go anywhere near it for the time being.'

'Understandably so. Any other less crazy techniques that I should be aware of?', Steven asked, noticing the sadness in his brother's voice.

'Hm...', Adrian thought. 'Ah, yes, I don't think I told you anything about bends. A bend is something you do by playing a note on a fret and then pushing the string with your fretting hand so that the pitch of the notes goes higher. I find it easier if I push the string with two fingers. It looks something like this on a tab:'

```
E|---12b14----------12^14--------------------|
B|-------------------------------------------|
G|-------------------------------------------|
D|-------------------------------------------|
A|-------------------------------------------|
E|-------------------------------------------|
```

'So there's two notations for this?'

'Yeah, though the first one is more common. Try it out'.

Steven then attempted to bend a note on his classical guitar. But after pushing his string to the point where his hand was actually hurting, he asked:

'So, how much do I have to push this string before I actually notice a change higher than a half-step?'

'Hm, I suppose it's useful for you to know that bending strings on an acoustic guitar or classical is harder than on an electric guitar. I usually jump to play the electric guitar whenever my teacher allowed me to, simply because the strings are so much softer on the fingers and I can bend strings quite easily.'

'Now that I think about it, I think I've encountered this technique mentioned in some articles regarding useful guitar techniques. They also mentioned something like pre-bending, which I assume you have to pre-bend the string before you play the note, which once again seems needlessly complicated', Steven added.

'That would be correct'.

'Ugh, I feel as though my head is about to explode. There's so much stuff going on here, it's really annoying. And hearing there are things which even you can't do is both relaxing and scary at the same time.'

'You've got to realize that there are some things which I am not accustomed to because I didn't care enough to get accustomed to them. It's all about patience, in the end, which you still need to learn.'

Steven conceded that his brother was correct. Patience had always been a department where he was lacking.

He was not ready to give up just yet, though he still felt that something was missing from all of this. He liked guitar, but deep down, his gut was telling him that this was not the role for him. However, he noticed the rise in Adrian's morale ever since they both started spending more time on their instruments and that was enough to keep him going, at least for now.

Chapter 11 – Sweep picking, vibrato and triplets

There was less than a month to go until school was going to start, and Steven was getting better and better at playing the guitar. He was getting so good that learning his favorite songs was getting easier by the day. It also helped that during this time, he did play alongside his brother, as a rhythm guitarist for the most part.

One day, Adrian noticed that his brother was sweeping the kitchen with a broom. At first, he did not look too much into this until Steven brought the broom next to his guitar.

'Ok, I'll take the bait. What is it that you're doing?'

'Trying to figure out how the sweeping motion from the broom can be used when playing guitar', Steven replied.

'I... You don't exactly understand what sweep picking actually means, do you?'

'So, it doesn't have anything to do with brooms?'

'No.'

'Oh, well, I feel a bit silly now', Steven laughed.

'Eh, it's fine. Let's go over the basics. This is one of the harder techniques, so be prepared to be annoyed, again and again.'

Adrian then looked through his notes and found the following tab:

```
E|--15p12--------------12--15p12-------------12------|
B|---------13------13------------13------13------13~-|
G|------------12-------------------12-------------|
D|--------------------------------------------------|
A|--------------------------------------------------|
E|--------------------------------------------------|
```

'So, what's so special about this technique?' Steven asked after playing it.

'It has to do with your picking hand movement. From what I can tell, you used alternate picking. The idea is that your picking hand needs to follow a seamless upward or downward movement, depending on where your notes are found.'

Adrian then picked up his guitar and continued.

'What was that wiggly sound at the end?' asked Steven.

'What even are those descriptions…that's called a vibrato. It's obtained by pushing and pulling the string really fast. Sort of like very fast and short bends. You get what I'm saying?'

'I think so. It's a really cool technique. So, what about this sweep picking?'

'Right, sweep picking and hand movement. For example, when you start the sequence above, you will notice that after the pull-off, both of the following notes are on lower strings than the first two. That means that the first four notes need to be played using upstrokes.'

'Upstrokes are the ones where the motion is towards my head, right?'

'Yeah.'

Steven then attempted to use upstrokes for the first four notes and then managed to play the following two with downstrokes.

'That's exactly the correct way of playing this!' exclaimed Adrian.

'Phew, I'm glad for that one at least. But from what I can tell, the next note on the 15th fret needs to be played with a downstroke as well. I have to switch to upstrokes again afterward, right?'

'Yeah, that's correct. That's the idea of sweep picking. Your picking hand needs to move up and down. The tricky part is to synchronize your hands. At slow speeds, that's not a problem, but at faster tempos, it is insanely difficult.'

'Seems like a fair assumption, what with everything I've been learning so far. You got another one of these?'

Adrian looked through his notes and found the following exercise:

```
E|--17p12---------------------12-17p12--|
B|-------13----------------13-----------|
G|----------14----------14--------------|
D|------------14----14------------------|
A|---------------15---------------------|
E|-------------------------------------|
```

'What in the name of... are you sure this can be played with only five fingers on each hand?' exclaimed Steven after attempting to play this.

'Just stretch that pinky finger a little bit more. Like this.'

Adrian then played back the sequence.

'Stretching it a little bit more is an understatement. But what was that waltz-y mood you did when playing those notes?'

'Those are called triplets. It's a special type of note length, fairly useful and widely used in rock and metal. And waltzes. Do you remember the note length equivalency?'

'Yeah, the whole quarter note is two eighth notes and so on?'

'Yeah, that. For triplets, that changes a bit. For example, a quarter note is split into three triplet eighth notes, rather than two. Basically, a triplet eighth note lasts one-third of a quarter note. The equivalency is the same for all other note lengths as well. In that, a double note consists of three triplet quarter notes, an eight note consists of three triplet 16th notes and so on.'

'Ok, seems fair. But given how you can group three notes like this, can it be done for more notes?'

'Yeah. Such groups are called tuplets. You can have quintuplets, sextuplets and so on. Triplets look like this:'

'I see. Makes sense so far. Got any tuplet examples?'

'Yeah, check them out:'

'I see. Going back a bit, these shapes that you have provided for sweep picking…they're movable, right? Meaning I can use them all around the fretboard so long as they fit the chords?'

'Exactly. What I've shown you are a C major and an A minor forms.'

'I feel a brain freeze coming. I think we should stop here for today.'

'Seems fair. Got to keep some free space for all those free-flow combos in fighting games after all.'

'Yeah, I'm off those at the moment. They're way too annoying', added Steven.

'The game's AI still getting the better of you?'

'Now listen here, you little…'

The boys' discussion was interrupted by their mother telling them to get dressed because today was the day they were going to an adventure park.

Chapter 12 – Every note can be found anywhere on the guitar

As the summer was almost over, the boys were enjoying their last days of school break doing various activities. Adrian's mood had been improving as he started focusing more and more on improving his guitar skills. And while he was not at the level of the greats yet, he knew he'd get there one day.

As for Steven, he was enjoying the ride of learning the ropes behind playing this instrument. It opened his eyes to the idea of being a musician. It wasn't something he considered doing until he started playing guitar. And on that note, it appears he had one more question regarding this topic.

'So, I was wondering, is there any sort of way of playing a chord anywhere on the fretboard?' Steven asked his brother.

'What do you mean?'

'I mean, if I find myself on the 5th fret area for example, and I want to play a chord without using one of the predefined shapes we talked about until now. Can that be accomplished?'

'Oh, I get it now. Yeah, it can be done. The idea is that, regardless of where you find yourself on the guitar, you can find every possible note there.'

'Seems oddly convenient though', replied Steven.

'Yes and no. The first step is to understand how to look at the fretboard differently. And by differently, I mean in boxes of four frets on each string.'

Steven felt a bit confused by this.

'It's something like this', Adrian continued. 'Say you start on the 3rd fret on the low E string. If you were to use the notes on four consecutive frets on the low E string, you'd be using frets three, four, five, and six. This is the whole four-fret box idea in a nutshell, only expanded on all six strings.'

'Oh, so you mean I'd be using the notes on frets three, four, five, and six on the low E string, the A string, and so on?'

'Yeah, exactly. Here's how that looks like starting on the 3rd fret.'

Adrian then showed his brother the following picture:

Every note can be anywhere

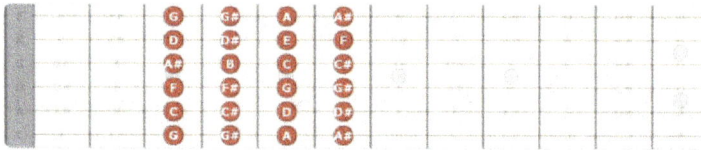

Steven looked at the picture.

'Huh, yeah, I get it now. I can actually see that all the notes are there. So, what do I do with this now?'

'Well, remember the relationship between chords and triads?'

'Yeah, technically, in order to play a chord, a triad is enough. So what, I just play a triad with the notes available in such a box?'

'That's exactly right. Try playing a D chord. In more ways than one.'

After some fiddling around with the shape, Steven came up with some interesting ways in which he could play a D chord:

```
E | ---5-------5--- |
B | ---3-------3--- |
G | -------------- |
D | ---4---4---4--- |
A | -------5---5--- |
E | -------5------- |
```

'Ugh, that last one is a bit stretchy. Is this how it's supposed to work?'

'Yeah, that's exactly right. And the technique can be used anywhere on the guitar. But you know, with the added info that the notes will be in a different order and stuff.'

'I get that. This one's really useful though. Like, it feels like I've found a secret level which is way cooler than the main campaign.'

Adrian thought for a bit and then said:

'That's actually a really good analogy.'

The boys spent the remainder of the school break doing jamming sessions, with Steven doing the rhythm part and Adrian doing lead. It was one of the best times they ever had, and both of them enjoyed those sessions to the fullest.

There were times when Steven would also do some singing, and Adrian noticed his brother had the vibe of an actual lead singer. And while his techniques could be improved, he couldn't help but notice how much he enjoyed the singing part.

Adrian once again remembered the high school band contest. Could participating in it be feasible now? He was secretly hoping Steven would love playing music. And now that that dream came true, he was hoping he would keep at it.

He would find out some answers soon enough, though. High school was just around the corner.

www.ingramcontent.com/pod-product-compliance
Lightning Source LLC
LaVergne TN
LVHW022011080426
835513LV00009B/670